**ART BOOKS**

FROM CRESCENT MOON PUBLISHING


*Leonardo da Vinci*
by James Pearson

*Early Netherlandish Painting*
by Rosalind Mutter

*Piero della Francesca*
by Naomi Haskell

*Giovanni Bellini*
by Julia Davis

*Eric Gill: Nuptials of God*
by Anthony Hoyland

*Minimal Art and Artists In the 1960s and After*
by Laura Garrard

*Postwar Art*
by George Knighton

*Vincent van Gogh: Visionary Landscapes*
by Stuart Morris

*Max Beckmann*
by Stuart Morris

*Egon Schiele: Sex and Death in Purple Stockings*
by D. Simon Eade

*Mark Rothko: The Art of Transcendence*
by Julia Davis

*Jasper Johns*
by L.M. Poole

*Brice Marden*
by Laura Garrard

*Frank Stella: American Abstract Artist*
by James Pearson

# Rembrandt van Rijn

# REMBRANDT VAN RIJN

BY
MALCOLM BELL
AUTHOR OF "SIR EDWARD BURNE-JONES:
A RECORD AND REVIEW," ETC.

CRESCENT MOON

First published 1901. This edition © 2018.

Printed and bound in the U.S.A.
Set in Book Antiqua 10 on 14pt.
Designed by Radiance Graphics.



*British Library Cataloguing in Publication data*

*ISBN-13 9781861716316*

*CRESCENT MOON PUBLISHING*
*P.O. Box 1312, Maidstone, Kent, ME14 5XU*
*Great Britain, www.crmoon.com*

# CONTENTS

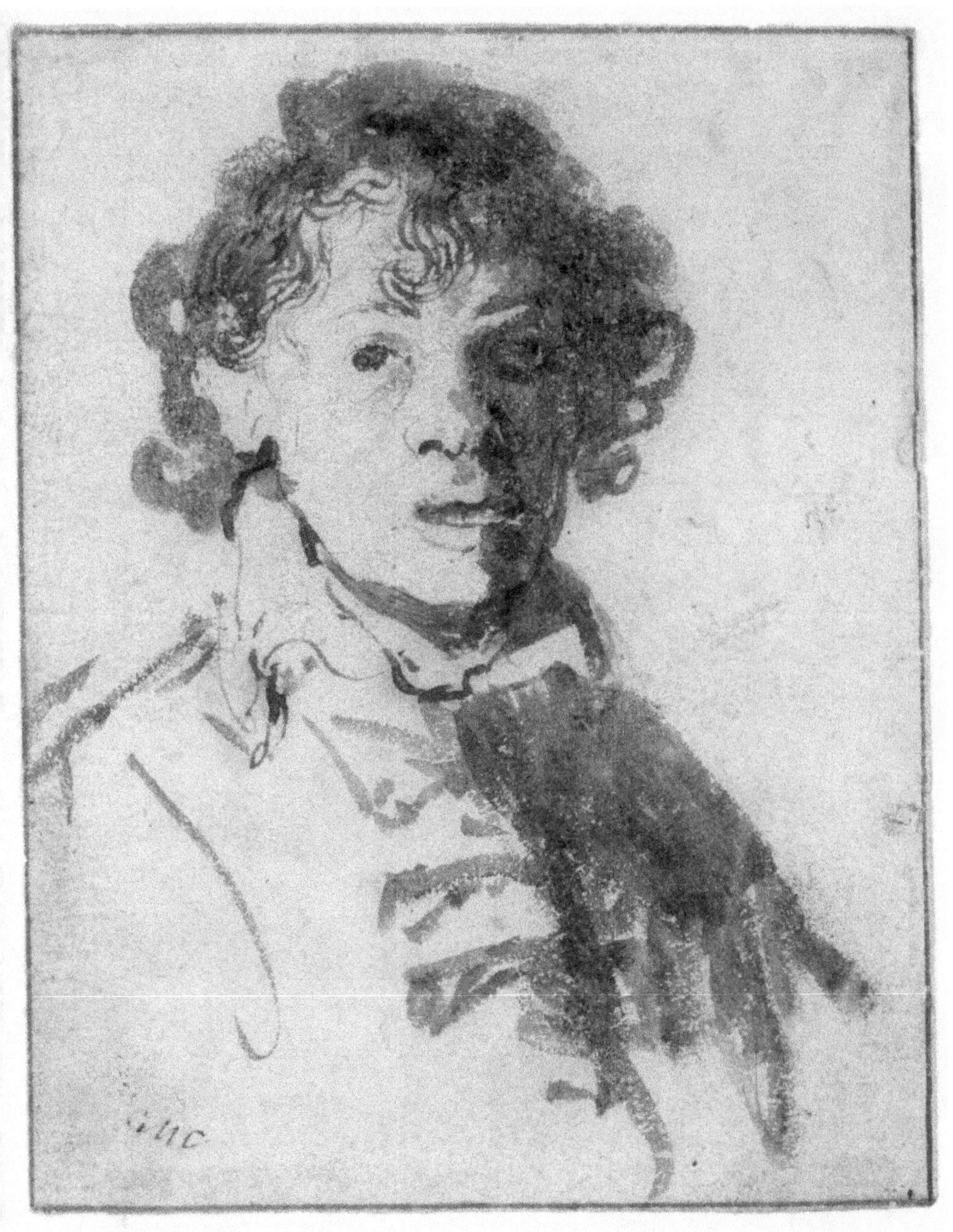

Rembrandt van Rijn, Self-Portrait With Open Mouth, 1629, British Museum

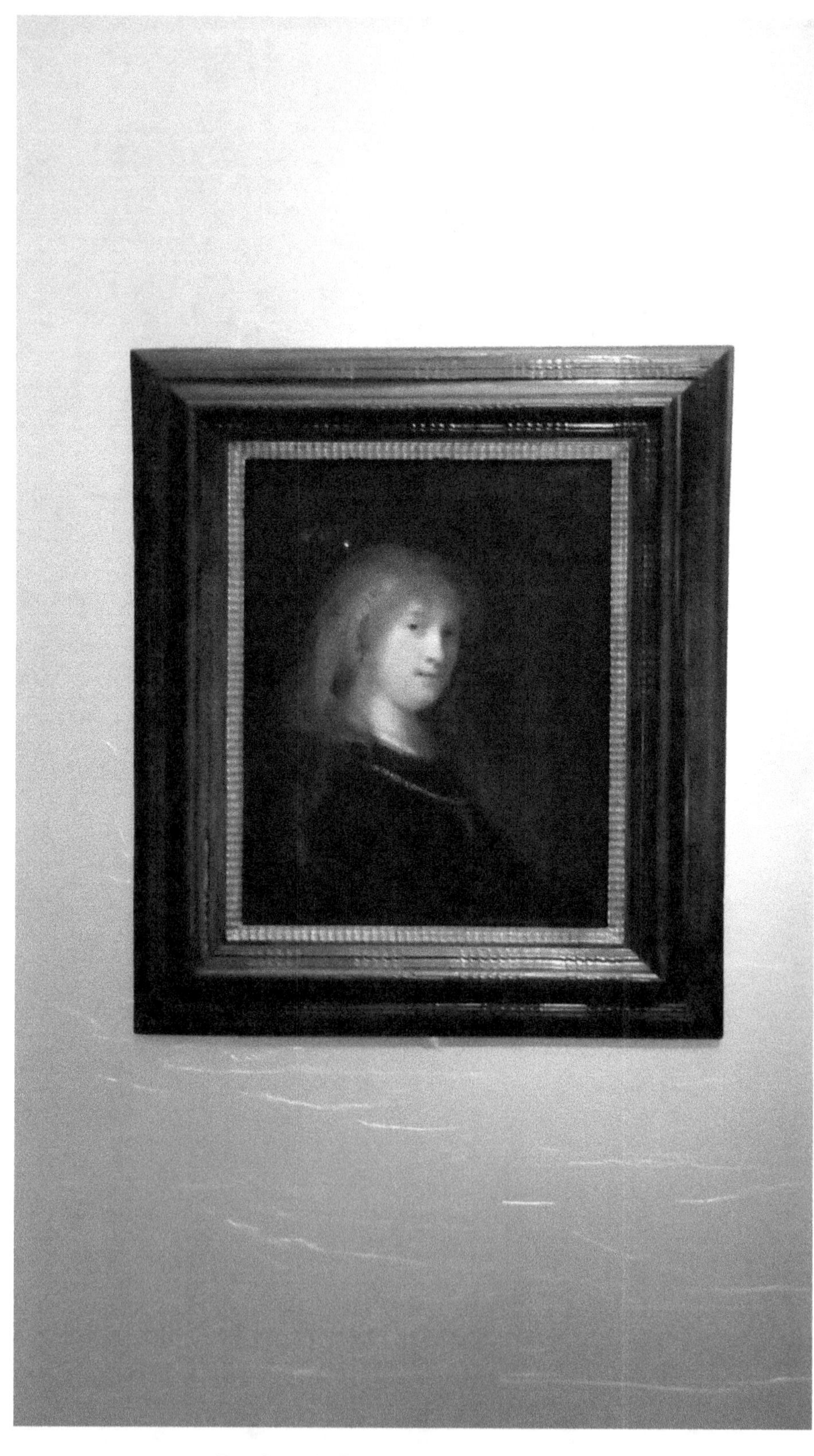

Rembrandt, Self-Portrait, Amsterdam

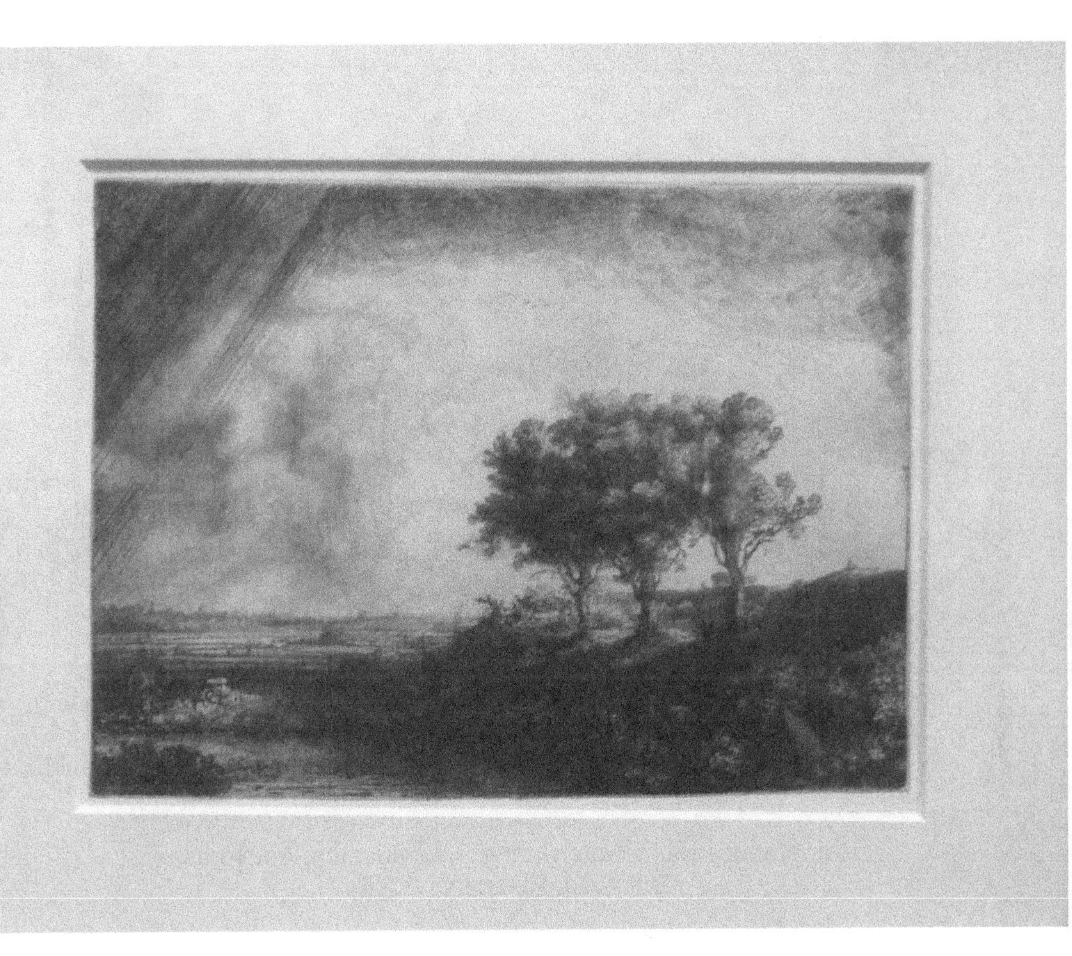

Rembrandt, Three Trees

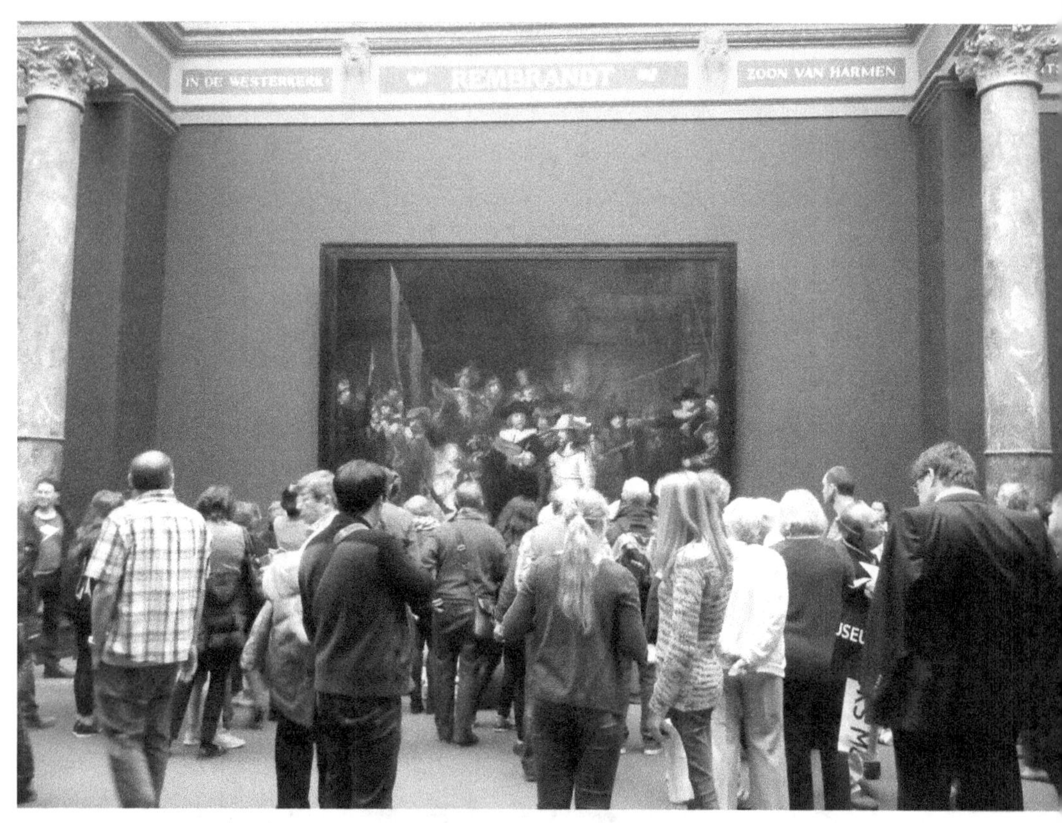


Rembrandt's Night Watch in the Rijksmuseum, Amsterdam
(photo: J. Robinson, 2015)

# PREFACE

In order to reduce the volume on Rembrandt, published in 1899, to the smaller dimensions demanded by the "Great Masters" series, it became necessary to dispense with some of the material included in it. This, it is hoped, has been done without seriously affecting the usefulness of the book. The story of the painter's life and work has been to some extent compressed, but everything essential has, it is believed, been retained. The chief omissions are the short descriptions of the pictures and the lists of the etchings, which, while occupying much space, were thought to be more suitable to a work of reference than to a handbook. The student who desires fuller information on these points will find it in the earlier volume.

# CHRONOLOGICAL TABLE

Year
Events in Rembrandt's Life
Principal Work Dated

1606
Born July 15th.

1620
Entered at Leyden University, and later Swanenburch's Studio.

1623
Went to Lastman's Studio.

1624
Returned to Leyden.

1627
First known pictures.
St Paul in Prison.

1628
Gerard Dou became his pupil.

Capture of Samson.

1629
Portrait of Himself (Gotha).

1630
His father died.
Joseph interpreting his Dreams.

1631
Left Leyden for Amsterdam.
Presentation in the Temple.

1632
Living on the Bloemgracht.
The Anatomy Lesson.

1633
Moved to Saint Anthonie's Breestraat (about).
The Shipbuilder and his Wife.

1634
Married on June 22nd.
Descent from the Cross (Hermitage).

1635
Rombertus born.
Abraham's Sacrifice.

1636
Living in Nieuwe Doelstraat.
Danae.

1637
Susannah at the Bath.

1638
Cornelia born.
Christ and Mary Magdalen.

1639
Moved to Jode-Breestraat.
Resurrection.

1640
His mother died.
Portrait of Elizabeth Bas.

1641
Titus born.
Portrait of Anslo.

1642
Saskia died.
The Night Watch.

1643
Bathsheba.

1644
Woman taken in Adultery.

1645
Holy Family (Hermitage).

1646
Finished two pictures for the Stathouder.
Adoration of the Shepherds.

1647
An estimate made of Saskia's property.

Susannah and the Elders.

1648
Christ at Emmaus.

1649
Hendrickje Stoffels first heard of.
No dated picture.

1650
Deposition.

1651
Noli me tangere.

1652
Hendrickje's first daughter born.
Portrait of Bruyningh.

1653
Borrowed money in large sums.
Portrait called Van der Hooft.

1654
Birth of second daughter, Cornelia.
Bathsheba (Louvre).

1655
Joseph accused by Potiphar's Wife.

1656
Declared bankrupt.
Parable of Labourers in the Vineyard.

1657
Sale of his property ordered.
Portrait of Catrina Hoogh.

1658
Pictures, etc., sold.
An Old Woman cutting her Nails.

1659
Jacob wrestling with the Angel.

1660
Association formed by Hendrickje and Titus.
Portrait of Himself (Louvre).

1661
The last known etching.
The Syndics.

1662
Hendrickje (probably) died.
No dated picture.

1663
Homer.

1664
Moved to the Lauriergracht.
Lucretia.

1665
Titus awarded his property.
Portrait of a Man (Metrop. Mus., New York).

1666
Portrait of J. de Decker.

1667
Portrait of an Old Man.

1668
Titus' marriage and death.
The Flagellation.

1669
Rembrandt died.
No dated picture.

# PART I

# REMBRANDT THE MAN

# CHAPTER I

# BIRTH AND EARLY YEARS

Down to the middle of the present century the story of Rembrandt, as generally accepted, was nothing but a mass of more or less ill-natured fiction. His drunkenness, his luxury, his immorality, his avarice, were heaped together into a somewhat inconsistent midden-heap of infamy. It was not indeed until his true rank among painters began to be properly appreciated that it occurred to anyone to ask whether this harsh judgment did not need revision; nay, more, to inquire upon what evidence it had been first delivered, and the investigation had not long been set on foot before the question took the form – "Is there any evidence, good or bad, at all?"

There were soon many workers in this untried field, and to all the thanks of the artist's admirers are due, but it is chiefly to M. Charles Vosmaer that his complete rehabilitation is to be credited, and it is bare justice to say that without availing himself freely of his researches and of M. Michel's equally careful and critical marshalling of the facts, then and since obtained by others, no future historian of Rembrandt can hope to advance beyond the threshold of his subject. One by one the cobwebs of myth with which, partly through malice, partly through ignorance, the master's image had been overwhelmed have been torn away, and we begin at last to see him as he really was, not impeccable, but intensely human, a kindly, patient, laborious, much-tried soul – one whom fortune, not altogether without his own provoking be it frankly owned, sorely buffeted, but one who, though well-nigh crushed, was never subdued; one whose courage sustained him to the last, whose one refuge against her flouts was in his art; who met, uncomplaining, neglect and contempt in his later years as he had in the heyday of his career received, unspoiled, unstinted praise and well-earned fame, and who said of himself in the height of his prosperity, "When I want rest for my mind, it is not honours I crave, but liberty."

Much concerning Rembrandt has been revealed by M. Vosmaer and his fellow-workers, by MM. Bredius and Scheltema, de Vries and Immerzeel, Elzevier and Eckhoff, van der Willigen, and other patient seekers, but much, nevertheless, still remains in doubt or darkness.

Even as to the date of his birth, there is considerable uncertainty. Orlers, a burgomaster of Leyden, in a description of that town published in 1641, and therefore while not only Rembrandt himself but many people who must have remembered his birth were still alive, states that Rembrandt, the son of Hermann, the son of Gerrit, and Neeltje, the daughter of Willems of Suydtbroeck, was born on the 15th of July 1606, and later writers for more than two hundred years accepted his assertion without question. Dr Bredius has, however, shown that on May 25th, 1620, Rembrandt was entered as a student in the Faculty of Letters at the University of Leyden and his age is given in the same document as fourteen, *Rembrandt Hermanni Leidensis 14 jare oud*, and as this was before his birthday in that year the question arises as to whether the statement means that he was in his fourteenth year or that he had passed the fourteenth anniversary of his birthday. For, the day of his birth not being in dispute, if we take the latter and more obvious interpretation it would necessarily follow that the fourteenth anniversary was in

1619 and that he completed his first year on 25th May 1606, so that the actual day itself must have been in 1605. There is further and still conflicting evidence to be reckoned with. In the British Museum there is a proof of an etched portrait of himself dated 1631 [B. 7], on which is written, in what is believed to be his own hand, "*aet.* 24, 1631." If this was written before the 15th of July it would point to 1606 as his birth year, thus agreeing with Orlers' statement, while if it was written after that day it would imply 1607. It should, however, be observed that M. Blanc reads the figures on the etching as 25, and if he be correct in this the choice must lie between 1607 and 1608; while, to add further to the mystification, Mr Sidney Colvin reads the age as 27, which makes the birth year 1603 or 1604.

Nor is 1607 without further support. Dr Scheltema discovered in the marriage register of Amsterdam the record of Rembrandt's official engagement to duly obtain his mother's consent to his marriage, signed by himself, and in this he gives his age on July 10th, 1634, as twenty-six, in which case his birthday would have fallen in 1607, but we know that he was at all times very vague as to dates and figures. On a delightful pencil drawing on vellum, in the Berlin Museum, of his wife Saskia, there is an inscription in his handwriting "Dit is naer myn huysfrow geconterfeit do sy 21 jaer oud was den derden dach als wy getroudt waeren due 8 junyus 1633" – "This is a portrait of my wife when she was 21 years old, on the third day after our marriage, the 8th of June 1633," a simple statement, which nevertheless contains a remarkable number of errors for so brief a document. Saskia, it is true, was twenty-one in 1633, but the marriage took place on the 22nd of June and in the year 1634.

If, then, Rembrandt could misdate an event so intimately connected with his life's chief joy, how should we expect him to be more accurate about one, which indeed concerned him nearly, but of which he naturally had no personal recollection. That he was uncertain we have happily positive proof, thanks once more to Doctor Bredius, for on the 16th of September 1653, in giving his opinion as an expert in a trial concerning the authenticity of a certain picture by Paul Bril, he can only declare that he is about forty-six.

Such is the evidence upon this fortunately not very important point, and it is small wonder that of the two great authorities, M. Michel and M. Vosmaer, the first accepts 1606 and the second 1607 as the true date. The question must still remain an open one, but when we consider that Rembrandt's mother did not die until 1640, only one year before Orlers published his book, and at a time when he had probably collected most of his material, and that nothing is more likely than that he should have applied to her for details, we may with safety conclude that the balance of probability is in favour of his date 1606.

Concerning the place of his birth there are no such doubts. If the visitor to Leyden, on his way from the station to the town, turns sharp to the right after crossing the second bridge, and on traversing a third keeps again to the right and continues with that branch of the Rhine known as the Galgewater on his right hand, he will before long find himself on the west side of the town, in a triangular open space, washed on two sides by the moat surrounding it, where once stood the White Gate guarding the entrance of the high-road from the Hague. On the left side of this, as one comes in from the country, and at right angles to it, close to where the buildings of the Zeemans-Kweekschool, or Naval School, now are, ran a short street called the Weddesteeg, in No. 3 of which Rembrandt was born.

It must have been a pleasant situation, facing the setting sun, with nothing but the town ramparts and the gleaming moat between it and the wide champaign. On the right hand the slow barges crept up and down the river, on the left the slow carts creaked to and from the town, while in front the broad sails of windmills swung round, and the whirr of the stones grinding malt for making beer hummed through the open doors. Up against the sky rose two, one almost opposite the windows of the house, the other a little to the left on the border of the

Noordeinde, just inside the gate, of which Rembrandt's father owned half, while his stepfather Cornelis, the son of Clæs, with his son Clæs, shared the other half between them.

He was a prosperous and respected man was Hermann, or Harmen – the name occurs in both forms – the son of Gerrit, called after the fashion of the time Harmen Gerritsz, to which he himself added van Rijn, as his son did after him. Besides his own residence, and his share of the mill, he owned houses within the town and gardens without, with plate and jewellery and house-plenishings and all things proper about him, and had been appointed by his fellow-citizens to a municipal office of importance, representing the ward of the Pelican, in which he lived, where he did so well what was asked of him that he was selected again for it some years later. He was at the former date thirty-five or thirty-six, and at the time when this, his fifth and youngest child but one, was born, he had been married fifteen years, his wedding-day having been the 8th of October 1589.

Rembrandt's childhood, considering the condition of his father, was, we may be sure, at least a comfortable one, though of details we have none. We cannot even say where he learned to read and write, for neither of which exercises did he subsequently exhibit much affection. Probably at home, where maybe Coppenol, the great master of writing, at that time included among the fine-arts under the style of Caligraphy, taught him, and possibly gave him his first lessons in drawing also; for the art he professed, with its elaboration of curves and flourishes, and its, to our eyes, somewhat childish pictorial perversions, was a singular commingling of the two. One thing at least we may feel certain of, that it was at his mother's knee he began the study of the Bible, which she herself read so constantly, if we may judge by its frequent appearance in his portraits of her, and which he, following in her footsteps, knew so thoroughly and drew upon so often for inspiration.

The next fact we find chronicled is a passage in Orlers to the effect that his parents sent him to school to learn the Latin tongue, in preparation for the University of Leyden, that when he came of age he might by his knowledge serve the City and Republic; and in fulfilment of this laudable ambition we find that entry on May 25th, 1620, as a student in the Faculty of Letters, which has already been noted in another connection. But by this time, by what means we know not, the art craving was fully aroused, and his parents' ambitious scheme for his serving the City and Republic was as nothing beside his own irresistible desire to express himself in form and colour. He proved, we are told, but an unwilling scholar, the lines of Virgil and Ovid were lifeless to him, in comparison with those of Lucas van Leyden; and his elders, yielding with a fortunate wisdom to the inevitable, gave up the effort to make a statesman of him, and consented to apprentice him, according to his wish, to a painter to learn first principles from him.

# CHAPTER II

# ART EDUCATION
# AND EARLY WORKS

The exact date of this first step on the road to fame is also still somewhat uncertain. Vosmaer believes it was in 1619, but the assertion of Orlers that when his parents allowed him to abandon the unloved Latin, they apprenticed him to a painter, is so precise, that it is unreasonable to suppose that his father should have returned to the attack. We may consequently assume that the final desertion of the Muses and enlistment in the cause of the Arts came after, not before, that enrolment at the University – that is to say, late in 1620 or perhaps early in 1621. Further facts go to prove this point. His first apprenticeship, in accordance with the rules of the Guilds of Saint Luke, lasted three years, and came to an end therefore in 1623 or early in 1624. He then went to a second master in Amsterdam, but remained with him only six months; so that in either case the date of his leaving Amsterdam and returning to Leyden would have been some time in 1624. Now there is no doubt that it was in 1624 that this took place, and the only obvious conclusion is that his first apprenticeship did not commence before 1620.

The painter who was then chosen for the honour of first

guiding the hand of the young Rembrandt, by which honour he is nowadays almost alone distinguished, was Jacob van Swanenburch. A man of good position, the son of one painter, the brother of another, and of an engraver, he was not, judging by his only known picture, "A Papal Procession in the Piazza of St Peter," artistically speaking, of much account, and it was probably more for personal reasons, and because of his propinquity, than for his conspicuous talents that he was selected. He was able only to impart "the first elements and the principles" of his art to his young pupil, as Orlers tells us; but indeed these were all that were needed by one with such an overmastering personality, with so powerful an artistic inspiration and energy. So successful was the process that Orlers describes his advance in craftsmanship as so swift and steady that his fellow-citizens were completely astounded by it, and could already foresee the brilliant career to which he was destined. We must, however, remember in weighing this statement that it was written when that career was at its most brilliant stage, and is to some extent the proverbial safe prophecy of one who knows.

That Rembrandt did make considerable progress during the following three years is, of course, certain; and when his apprenticeship drew to an end the question arose as to what was to come next. The experience of a young fellow-artist probably suggested the answer. About the time Rembrandt entered Swanenburch's studio Jan Lievensz, a fellow-citizen, a year younger than Rembrandt, who had, however, entered upon his artistic studies while Rembrandt was still struggling with, or against, the detested Latin, returned from completing his studies in the studio of Pieter Lastman at Amsterdam. The father of Jan was a farmer, a man in the same rank of life as Hermann the miller, and probably had business connections with him, so that the acquaintanceship between the two sons, destined to ripen into warm friendship, doubtless began in early boyhood.

Certain it is, at any rate, that when Jan returned from Lastman's studio to astound his townsmen with his precocity, the intimacy between him and Rembrandt became close; in a few years their names seem to have become as inseparable as those of Damon and Pythias, and it was no doubt from the enthusiasm of Lievensz that the impulse arose which, in 1624, sent Rembrandt also to study under Lastman. The experiment, however, was not a success. Lievensz had remained with him two years; Rembrandt wearied of it in six months. And, truly, though he enjoyed at that time an incomprehensibly large measure of popularity and success, Lastman, though a far better artist than Swanenburch, was not one of those whose names we nowadays inscribe on the roll of great painters. He had been, moreover, one of the large group who had trudged to far-away Rome, and come under the influence of Elsheimer there, and the exotic and ill-adapted traditions and conventions of the school were not calculated to appeal to so ardent and eager a seeker after truth as Rembrandt. He wanted to find nature, and was not to be put off by a diluted semi-Italian imitation of it; and so, after a few months' trial, he packed up his paints and canvases, and returned to his family in Leyden "to study and practise painting alone and in his own way," to quote again the garrulous Orlers.

That so indefatigable and untiring a worker as Rembrandt did not waste time, when once he was safely established in his father's house, is certain, for Orlers says that he worked incessantly as long as the light lasted; but we know of nothing that he produced until three years later, when he painted two still existing pictures, signing and dating both.

From this time his reputation and that of Lievensz ripened rapidly. Arent van Buchel, in his "Res Pictoriæ," mentions him in 1628; and Constantin Huygens, in a manuscript autobiography, discovered in 1891 by Dr Worp of Groningen, and written probably between 1629 and 1631, was enthusiastic concerning both, "still beardless yet already famous" – an appreciation that was not to be without its favourable influence on Rembrandt's future. Nor was this growing fame productive of mere empty praise. In February 1628, when he was only one-and-twenty,

Gerard Dou, his first pupil, came to him and remained until he left Leyden for Amsterdam three years later.

Many causes probably combined to promote this change of residence. On the twenty-seventh of April 1630 the first break in the united family circle was brought about by the death of his father. The blow must have been a heavy one, for he must have been a kindly and sympathetic companion to his children, if we may judge by the refined and sensitive face which looks out at us from the portraits believed to be his, and a merry one to boot, with a pretty humour of his own, if M. Michel be justified in his conclusion that the etching of the bald man with a chain (B. 292) is also a portrait of him. The loss further brought changes into the family arrangements. The eldest brother, as far back as 1621, had been crippled by an accident, and on March 16th of that year a life-interest in the estate to the amount of 125 florins per annum had been formally established for his maintenance, so that the superintendence of the affairs of the mill fell to the second son Adriaen, who abandoned his trade of shoe-making to undertake it, and made nothing, or worse, of it.

The young artist's reputation as a portrait painter had, moreover, spread to Amsterdam some time before, and many commissions came to him thence. For a while he merely went over, stayed long enough to do the work, and returned again to Leyden, but as the demands upon his time increased this must have proved a wasteful, inconvenient, and finally impossible proceeding. Leyden, again, was a University town, where religion and philosophy were more thought of and more sought after than such a trifle as art, as indeed is still the case in some University towns that could be mentioned; while Amsterdam was a city of prosperous traders making more money than they knew how to spend or employ, and ready enough to devote some of their superfluity to portraits of themselves and wives, or pictures of incidents and places, and it was clearly desirable that one able and willing to satisfy their wishes in this respect should be upon the spot.

The little coterie of artists, too, was on the verge of dispersal in any case, by the loss of Rembrandt's closest tie with it, Jan Lievensz. He had sold a picture of a man reading by a turf fire to the Prince of Orange, who had presented it to the English Ambassador, and he in turn had passed it on to that king of picture lovers, Charles the First, who had been so well pleased with it that a pressing invitation to visit England had been sent to the painter, and accepted. Nor, probably, was it only the chance of obtaining more employment that attracted Rembrandt. The famous "Anatomy Lesson" bears the date 1632, and, even if the commission for it had not actually been offered during the preceding year, it may very well have been suggested in the course of conversation by the doctor who had added to his name, Claes Pietersz, that of Tulp, taking it from a tulip which was carved on the front of his house, who figures so conspicuously in it. If this were so, it must have been evident to Rembrandt that to undertake so large and important a picture while living in another city would mean either risking the uniformity and continuity of his work, or settling down for a prolonged period in lodgings in Amsterdam, and this may well have confirmed his decision to at once establish himself there permanently.

Finally, I like to fancy, though it certainly cannot be proved, that Rembrandt had already, in one of his flying visits to that city, met the girl upon whom, while she lived, the larger part of his life's happiness was to depend. The evidence is, it must be owned, slight, but is not altogether wanting. Among the pictures of the year 1630, and, according to M. Michel, even of 1628 and onwards, we find a series of portraits of a fair-haired girl with a round, full forehead, and rather small eyes and mouth, which Dr Bode believes to be portraits of the painter's sister Lysbeth, while M. Michel considers that some of the later ones are really portraits of Saskia, urging the objection that many of them were undoubtedly painted after his removal to Amsterdam, whither there is not the slightest reason to suppose that Lysbeth accompanied him, what evidence there is pointing directly to the contrary. On the other hand, M. Michel admits that the type which is known to be Saskia blends almost indistinguishably with that supposed to be Lysbeth, and offers the distinctly dubious explanation that Rembrandt was, so to speak, so imbued with the features of his sister that he unconsciously transferred them to a large extent to the girl he loved. If, however, as we may quite reasonably suppose, Rembrandt had met and admired Saskia during his first stay in Amsterdam, and continued to do so during his after-visits, the occurrence of her features in his work would be what we ought to expect.

There was, on the other hand, but a single objection to the scheme – the parting with his mother; and to such an affectionate and home-loving nature as Rembrandt's the difficulty can have been no small one. Still, a man has to do a man's work in this life. Adriaen, his brother, and Lysbeth, his sister, were there to minister to her comfort, while Amsterdam was no great distance away; and though, doubtless, it was not altogether without tears that the widowed Neeltje consented to the departure of her youngest son, the decision was taken, and the consent yielded at last.

Indeed, it was inevitable that so great and, at one time, so popular an artist should, sooner or later, gravitate to the capital of his country; for, since the decay of Antwerp, Amsterdam was without a rival in the world for prosperity – the head-centre of commerce, the hub of the trade-universe. Sir Thomas Overbury, in 1609, describes it as surpassing "Seville, Lisbon, or any other mart town in Christendom." Evelyn, writing in 1641, says in his diary, "that it is certainly the most busie concourse of mortalls now upon the whole earth and the most addicted to com'erce."

Neither tempest nor battle could check her energy; and throughout the long desultory war from 1621 to 1648 between Spain and Holland, her traders hurried to and from the enemy's ports, supplying her even with the very munitions of war to carry on the contest; while for all this accumulated wealth there was but a limited outlet. Necessities being superabundant, it must be either hoarded or expended on luxuries, and among these pictures held high place. Quoting once more from Evelyn, we find him writing on August 13th, 1641: "We arrived late at Roterdam, where was their annual marte or faire, so furnished with pictures (especially Landskips and Drolleries, as they call those clounish representations), that I was amaz'd. Some I bought and sent into England. The reson of this store of pictures and their cheapness proceedes from their want of land to employ their stock, so that it is an ordinary thing to find a common Farmer lay out two or three thousand pounds in this comodity. Their houses are full of them, and they vend them at their faires to very great gaines." So, for a time, the Dutch painters drove a thriving trade; and as Amsterdam was by far the richest city, to Amsterdam the successful painter must needs repair.

# CHAPTER III

# DAYS OF PROSPERITY

Some time then in 1631 the die was cast, and the removal accomplished. There is reason to believe that he went at first to stay or lodge with Hendrick van Uylenborch, a dealer in pictures and other objects of art. Among his first proceedings on his arrival, was one sufficiently characteristic of him and destined to be repeated only too often in the future. He lent Hendrick money, one thousand florins, to be repayable in a year with three months' notice. Soon after, if not before, this indiscreet financial operation, as it proved later, he found the suitable residence he had meanwhile been seeking, on the Bloemgracht, a canal on the west side of the town, running north-east and south-west between the Prinsen Gracht and the Lynbaan Gracht, in a district, at that time on the extreme outskirts of the town, known as the Garden, from the floral names bestowed upon its streets and canals.

Here he settled to his work, and here in a short time fortune came to him. The enthusiasm aroused by "The Anatomy Lesson," when it was finished and hung in its predestined place in the little dissecting-room or Snijkamer of the Guild of Surgeons in the Nes, near the Dam, was immediate and immense. The artist leapt at once into the front rank, and became the fashionable portrait painter of the day. From three portraits, other than those of his own circle, painted in 1631, and ten in 1632, the number rose to forty between that year and 1634; or, taking all the surviving portraits between 1627 and 1631, we have forty-one, while from the five following years, from 1632 to 1636, there are one hundred and two. Commissions, indeed, flowed in faster than he could execute them, so Houbraken assures us, and the not infrequent occurrence of a pair of portraits, husband and wife, one painted a year or more after the other, tends to confirm this; so that those who wished to be immortalised by him had often to wait their turn for months together, while all the wealth and fashion of the city flocked to the far-off studio in the outskirts, the more fortunate to give their sittings, the later comers to put down their names in anticipation of the future leisure. From the beginning, too, pupils came clamouring to his doors, Govert Flinck and Ferdinand Bol, Philips Koninck, Geerbrandt van den Eeckhout, Jan Victors, Leendeert Cornelisz, and others, eager to pay down their hundred florins a year, as Sandrart says they did, and work with and for the lion of the day.

Not Fortune alone, however, with her retinue of patrons, and Fame, with her train of pupils, sought him out; Love, too, came knocking at his portal, and won a prompt admission. To the many admirable works produced at this time I shall return later, but three of those painted in 1632 call for further notice now. One is an oval picture, belonging to Herr Haro of Stockholm, representing the half-length figure of a girl in profile, facing to the left, fair-haired, and pleasant-looking rather than pretty; the second, in the Museum at Stockholm, shows us the same girl in much the same position, but differently dressed; while the third, in the collection of Prince Liechtenstein at Vienna, is a less pleasing representation of her in full face, wherein the tendency to stoutness and the already developing double chin detract from the piquancy of her expression and make her look more than her actual age, which we know to have been twenty at the time that these were painted.

We have heard her name casually already, in connection with the arrangements for Rembrandt's marriage, when discussing the date of his birth – for this is Saskia van Uylenborch, a cousin of his friend Hendrick, which fact may haply have had something to do with that ready loan of a thousand florins. Though poor Rembrandt, be it said, was, unhappily for him, never backward with loan or gift when he had money to give or lend. Saskia was born in 1612 at Leeuwarden, the chief town of Friesland in the north, across the Zuider Zee, and at the time when Rembrandt met her was an orphan, her mother, Sjukie Osinga, having died in 1619, and her father, Rombertus, a distinguished lawyer in his native place, in 1624. The family left behind was a large one, consisting, besides Saskia, of three brothers, two being lawyers and one a soldier, and five sisters, all married, who, as soon as the worthy Rombertus was laid to rest, seem to have begun wrangling among themselves concerning the estate; the quarrel, chiefly, as it appears, being sustained by the several brothers-in-law, and leading shortly to an appeal to law.

Among the less close relations was a cousin Aaltje, who was married to Jan Cornelis Sylvius, a minister of the Reformed Church, who, coming from Friesland, had settled in Amsterdam in 1610, and with them Saskia was in the habit of coming to stay. Where and when Rembrandt first met her we do not know. Probably at the house of Hendrick; it may have been, as has been said, in 1628 or earlier, for, if the acquaintance began in 1631, it ripened rapidly. Without accepting unhesitatingly all M. Michel's identifications of her, not only in portraits and studies but in subjects, such as that one which is known as "The Jewish Bride," now in the collection of Prince Liechtenstein, there is no question that she sat to him several times during the two years 1632 and 1633. The attraction was mutual; Rembrandt soon became a welcome visitor to the Sylvius household, and, in token doubtless of the kindness and hospitality which he there met with, he etched, in 1634, a portrait of the good old minister (B. 266).

The course of true love in this case ran smoothly enough; the young people soon came to an understanding; no difficulties were raised by Sylvius, who acted as Saskia's guardian; and the marriage was only deferred till Saskia came of age. The union, indeed, from a worldly point of view, was unexceptionable. Saskia, it is true, was of a good family, while Rembrandt sprang from the lower middle class, but he had already carved out for himself a rank above all pedigrees. Saskia was twenty, and he, with all his fame, was only twenty-six. The wedding, then, was decided on, and Rembrandt, painting Saskia yet again, put into her hands a sprig of rosemary, at that time in Holland an emblem of betrothal. It was possibly even fixed for some date late in 1633, when Saskia would have passed her twenty-first birthday.

Just at this time, to confirm, if that had been needed, Rembrandt's increasing reputation and prospects of future prosperity, he was brought into business relations with the chief personage in the land, Prince Frederick-Henry, who in 1625, on the death of his brother Maurice, had succeeded to the office of Stathouder, as the head of the Republic was officially entitled. Constantin Huygens, whose earlier enthusiasm for Rembrandt's work we have already noted, was the Prince's Secretary, acting in that quality as intermediary in his many dealings with artists, and clearly found time in the intervals of his duties to continue his acquaintance with Rembrandt. It was probably on his recommendation that the artist had painted in 1632 the portrait of his brother Maurice, and it was certainly at his suggestion that the Stathouder bought "The Raising of the Cross," now at Munich. Rembrandt, indeed, says as much in a letter to Huygens, still existing in the British Museum, in which he invites him to come and inspect the companion picture, "The Descent from the Cross," for which, though offering to leave it to the Prince's generosity, he considers two hundred livres would be a reasonable price. The picture was bought, and so content was the Prince with his purchase that soon afterwards he commissioned three other pictures to complete the set. The exact date of this event is unknown, but it cannot have been long delayed, for, in a letter written early in 1636 the painter informs Huygens that one of the three, "The Ascension," is finished and the other two half done.

With such guarantees of continued good fortune, there was nothing, when Saskia was once of age, to necessitate longer delay, in the completion of his happiness, but in the autumn she was peremptorily called away to Franeker, a town in Friesland, between Leeuwarden and the sea, where her sister Antje, the wife of Johannes Maccovius, professor of Theology, was lying ill, and where, on November the ninth, she died. This untoward occurrence put an end to the possibility of an immediate marriage, and Saskia went to spend the winter with another sister, Hiskia, who was married to Gerrit van Loo, a secretary of the government, and lived at Sainte Anne Parrochie, in the extreme north-west of Friesland; while Rembrandt, discontentedly enough, no doubt, toiled through the long winter months in his studio at Amsterdam.

In the spring of 1634, however, the sunshine returned again into his life, and he commemorated the advent, appropriately enough, by painting the bringer of it in the guise of Flora. The period of mourning was now at an end, and some time in May, probably, Saskia once more returned to Hiskia's to make preparation for the approaching day; while Sylvius, as her representative, and Rembrandt began to arrange the more formal business matters. On June 10th, as recorded by Dr Scheltema, Sylvius, as the bride's cousin, engaged to give full consent before the third asking of the banns; while Rembrandt, on his part, promised to obtain his mother's permission. Whether he merely wrote to Leyden for this, or whether, as is more probable, he went in person, we do not know; but in either case he wasted no time, for on the fourteenth he produced the necessary documents, and prayed at the same time that the formal preliminaries might be cut as short as possible. His appeal was evidently received with favour, for eight days later, on June 22nd, at Bildt, in the presence of Gerrit and Hiskia van Loo, he was duly married, first by the civil authorities, and afterwards by the minister Rodolphe

Hermansz Luinga in the Anna-kerk.

As far as domestic happiness depending upon their relations with one another went, there is every reason to suppose that this union was a thoroughly successful one; but we cannot help, nevertheless, feeling some doubts as to whether it was altogether the best that might have been for Rembrandt. Frank and joyous, but strong-willed, not to say obstinate, recklessly generous and prodigal, and without a thought for what the future might bring forth, he needed some firm yet tender hand to check, without seeming too much to control, his lavish impulses. Impossible to drive, yet easy enough to lead, a giant in his studio, a child in his business relations with the world outside its doors, he should have found some steady practical head to regulate his household affairs and introduce some order and economy into his haphazard ways. Such, unfortunately for him in the end, Saskia was not. Devoted to him, she yielded in everything, and his will was her law. As her love for him led her to let him do always as he would, so his passion for her led him to shower costly gifts upon her – pearls and diamonds, gold-work and silver-work, brocades and embroideries; nothing that could serve to adorn her was too good or too expensive. She would have been as happy in plain homespun, as long as he was there; but to give largely was in the nature of the man, and the very fortune that she brought with her was an evil, even at the time, in that it led him to further extravagances, while in the future it proved a still more serious one.

Furthermore, Rembrandt, hot-headed and impetuous as he was, must needs fling himself into the family quarrels and suits-at-law, taking therein the part of the one who had stood by him and Saskia at the altar, Gerrit van Loo, in whom, though he had possibly never set eyes on him till he went north to his wedding, he had already developed so complete a confidence that, exactly one month later, on July 22nd, as Dr Scheltema discovered, he gave him a full power of attorney to act for him in all affairs connected with the property in Friesland. From this sudden and violent partisanship still more trouble arose in due course, owing largely to the fact that his championship of Gerrit was soon after justified by his winning one of the many cases brought before the court of Friesland in the course of the prolonged dispute.

For the time, however, there is no doubt their happiness was supreme, and if for her sake he was energetically brewing the storm that was to burst upon him later, there were as yet no threatening clouds upon the horizon. Nor, be it said, was it on her account alone that he scattered money broadcast. The impulse to collect works of art, pictures, engravings, casts and statues, armour and curious objects, had begun to influence him even in early days at Leyden, and had become by that time a perfect mania. On February 22nd, 1635, we find his name as a purchaser at the Van Sommeren sale, and thereafter he reappears again and again as buyer at various auctions. But not even in this could he attempt to be business-like. Baldinucci, a Florentine, in a volume published in 1686, gives many interesting details anent Rembrandt, which he obtained at first hand from one of his later pupils, Bernard Keilh, a Dane, and among them relates that, when at a sale he saw anything he coveted, he ran it up in one bid to a wholly impossible price, thus making sure of it, and at the same time, as he explained, paying honour to his art.

The Van Uylenborch family quarrels happily did not extend to the sisters, amongst whom the most amicable relations appear to have prevailed. At any rate, in the summer of 1635, we find Saskia revisiting Sainte Anne Parrochie, to be with Hiskia during her confinement, and subsequently at the baptism of the child, a mark of kindly feeling the more notable in that she herself was about to become a mother. In the early winter, having returned meanwhile to her home, she gave birth to a son, who, on December 15th, in the Oudekerk, was christened Rombertus, after her father. Rembrandt's delight in this small person is indicated by numerous sketches of him and his mother; but the happiness, like all that he experienced, was short-lived, for the child did not long survive its birth.

☆ 42

Rembrandt, at some time before his marriage, had removed from the Bloemgracht to Saint Antonies Breestraat, in the heart of the city, close to the Nieuwe Markt, and by 1636 had moved once more to the Nieuwe Doelstraat, whence the letter to Huygens, already referred to, was addressed. There can be no doubt that the change was an improvement, for the artist must then have been at the height of his prosperity and fame.

Throughout Holland, imitators of his style were springing up, for the public would have no other. His studio was freely sought by pupils; his home-life was passed in a circle of trusted friends, and the broadly sympathetic nature of the man, which aided so largely in raising him to the first place among portrait painters, is seen in the various pursuits of these.

Fellow-painters, apart from his pupils, were not conspicuous among them, and those we find are chiefly landscape painters – Roghman and van der Helst, Ruysdael and Berchem, van de Cappelle and Jan Asselyn. With ministers he was largely acquainted, probably through Jan Sylvius, who, however, died on November 19th, 1638, among them being Alenson, Henry Swalm, and Anslo; while Tulp probably first introduced the medical element, Bonus, van der Linden, and Deyman. Several dealers in objects of art, brought in by Hendrick van Uylenborch, or picked up in the course of business transactions, were among his friends – Pieter de la Tombe, Clement de Jonghe, Abraham Francen, and others; while the worthy though conceited Coppenol, and the jeweller, Jan Lutma, together with the burgomaster Six, were among those who remained faithful to the last.

Rembrandt's championship of Gerrit van Loo in the family differences began about this time to bear troublesome fruit. The losers in the action already mentioned, in the course of the year 1634 seem to have nursed an especial grudge against Saskia, and, to relieve their ruffled feelings, had been spreading abroad reports reflecting on her, asserting that she had "dissipated her paternal inheritance in dress and ostentation." There was, as far as

Rembrandt himself, at least, was concerned, too much truth in the story to render the scandal altogether stingless. The thrust at Saskia, moreover, angered him more, probably, than one at himself alone would have done, and we find him accordingly rushing headlong into the law-courts with an action for damages against one Albert van Loo, declaring that "he and his wife were amply, even superabundantly, provided for."

Whether he was ever called upon to prove this statement does not appear; probably not, since the court found, in July 1638, that he had not sufficient grounds for action. It is doubtful how far he could have established its truth had he been required to do so. There can be small question that he believed it to be true, though his paying 637 florins the previous year for a book of drawings and engravings by Lucas van Leyden, and again, in October of the same year, 530 florins for a picture of Hero and Leander by Rubens, might only indicate his habitual indifference to ways and means. We know also that at the time he was getting from five to six hundred florins for his portraits, but, judging by the number known to exist – a very imperfect test it need scarcely be said – the demand for these was beginning to fall off, there being seven for 1636, four for 1637, two for 1638, and four for 1639, while even these small numbers include three of himself, and one believed to be his mother.

The strongest reason for supposing that he was in some financial embarrassment is found in his correspondence at the beginning of the latter year with Huygens. Writing in January from the Suijkerbackerij, a house on the borders of the Binnen-Amstel, whither he had removed at an unknown date, he announces the completion of the last two of the Stathouder's commissions, and only fifteen days later he presses for immediate payment of the 1244 florins due to him, on the grounds that the money would be then extremely useful to him. Since there was some delay, he renewed the appeal, though Huygens, on February 17th, had already given orders for the discharge of the debt. This unceremonious dunning, though by proxy, of a powerful Prince, does not seem altogether to indicate that superabundance of which Rembrandt boasted; but there was, as we know, a special reason, apart from any financial difficulties, which may have accounted for this urgent need of ready money.

He had decided to settle himself finally, not long after the birth on July 1st, 1638, of his second child, a daughter, christened at the Oudekerk on July 22nd, Cornelia, after his mother, and on January 5th, 1639, had purchased from one Christoffel Thysz a house in the Joden-Breestraat, now Number 68, for 13,000 florins. Though only one quarter of this sum had to be paid within one year, the rest being distributed over the following five or six, he seems for once to have been actually eager to pay the money, and by May had discharged half the cost and taken possession.

One birth and three deaths mark the year 1640. The first, of another daughter, on July 29th, who was also christened Cornelia, the elder child bearing that name having died in the meantime. The name, however, seems to have been an ill-omened one, for its second bearer did not survive a month, its burial being recorded in the Zuiderkerk on August 25th. Of the other deaths the first was that of an aunt of Saskia, who was possibly also her godmother, as she bore the same name, and certainly left her some property, since Ferdinand Bol was sent, on August 30th, to Leeuwarden with formal authority to take possession on her behalf. The other death must have been, to Rembrandt at any rate, a far heavier blow, for by it he lost, in September or October, his mother, to whom he was cordially attached, and from whom his residence in Amsterdam had only partially separated him, since we know by various portraits, painted subsequent to 1631, that either he visited her or she him with considerable frequency.

An event arising out of the consequent settlement of the estate has given rise to the suspicion that, then at all events, Rembrandt was in difficulties, but it is again possible to take another point of view. The inheritance of each child amounted to 2490 florins, and a further 1600 remained to be divided later. The business was entrusted to Adriaen and Lysbeth, and Rembrandt, unhesitatingly accepting every suggestion made by them, contented himself with a mortgage on half the mill, the redemption of which was to be postponed indefinitely. No sooner, however, was the arrangement completed than he authorised his brother Willem to sell his rights for what they would fetch. This may mean, as M. Michel supposes, that he wanted the money promptly, yet wished to deal tenderly with a brother who was himself by no means beforehand with the world; but the two reasons seem somewhat inconsistent with the facts. That Rembrandt, even though pressed for money himself, should have practically forgone his due, and consented to take a small annual interest which he could, in case necessity arose, easily forgo, is quite reconcilable with what we know of him; but that, having acted so, he should have at once undone the good he proposed, by selling his claim to some stranger, who would certainly demand the full letter of his bond, is hard to believe.

Any other evidence concerning these presumed embarrassments is certainly against them. At this very time he was cheerfully accepting security for considerable sums of money lent, in addition to the original one thousand florins, to Hendrick van Uylenborch; and in later years, when his affairs came to be inquired into, Lodewyck van Ludick and Adriaen de Wees, dealers both, swore that between 1640 and 1650 Rembrandt's collections, without counting the pictures, were worth 11,000 florins, while a jeweller, Jan van Loo, stated that Saskia had two large pear-shaped pearls, two rows of valuable pearls forming a necklace and bracelets, a large diamond in a ring, two diamond earrings, two enamelled bracelets, and various articles of plate. Finally, Rembrandt also, at a later date, estimated that his estate at the time of Saskia's death amounted to 40,750 florins; and though the estimate was made under circumstances calculated to incline him to exaggerate rather than diminish the amount, it must be considered as approximately correct.

Poor Saskia was not destined to enjoy much longer her plate and jewellery. Death, having entered the family, was thenceforth busy. Titia died at Flushing on June 16th, 1641; and Saskia herself, after the birth of Titus in September of that year, possibly never enjoyed really good health again. By the following spring she was unmistakably failing, and at nine in the morning of June 5th, 1642, she made her will. She was not even then without hope of recovery, for there are express stipulations as to any further children she might bear, but the pitiful irregularity of her signature at the end of the document shows how forlorn this hope was; and, in fact, she died within the following fortnight, and was buried on the 19th of June in the Oudekerk, where Rembrandt subsequently purchased the place of her sepulture.

Upon what this loss must have meant to Rembrandt, with his affectionate nature and almost morbid devotion to a home-life I need not dwell, nor did Fate rest content with dealing him this single blow. The great picture, which forms the chief ornament of the Ryksmuseum at Amsterdam, "The Sortie of the Company of Banning Cocq," better known under the inaccurate title of "The Night-Watch," was no sooner completed, in the course of the same year, than it aroused a storm of vituperative criticism. The reasons for this I must defer till I come to the consideration of the paintings, and must only note the fact here, and the dwindling of Rembrandt's popularity, which appears to have been, to some extent at least, the consequence.

One dim ray of consolation alone seems to beam through the darkness that overshadowed him, Lievensz, who had long been absent, first in England and subsequently in Antwerp, came to settle in Amsterdam, and doubtless did all that in him lay to comfort his doubly-stricken friend. In the meantime the business matters so loathed by him, and now aggravated by their intimate connection with his bereavement, had to be attended to, though, through the consideration of Saskia's relatives, they were made as easy for him as well might be. Saskia, by her will, left everything practically to Rembrandt, confident that he would properly educate Titus and start him in life. Ostensibly, indeed, her share of the estate was left to Titus and any other children she might bear, but she expressly stipulated that he was not to be asked to provide any inventory or guarantees to anyone whatsoever. She particularly forbade the interference of any Chamber of Orphans, in especial that at Amsterdam. Rembrandt alone was to have control, and the property, principal and interest, was to all intents his own, unless – an important exception as we shall find – he married again. In that case half of the joint estate at the time of her death was to be put in trust for the child or children, though Rembrandt was still to enjoy the interest for life. It was obvious that the making at once of an inventory of all the property in his possession was the only right course to pursue, in order that the share which might eventually revert to Titus should be accurately known, for Rembrandt was but six-and-thirty, and his re-marriage by no means impossible. He, however, wished to avoid this course, doubtless through that over-mastering distaste for business to which I have had and shall have occasion to refer so often, and having the consent of Hendrick van Uylenborch, obtained permission from the Chamber of Orphans, on December 19th, to enter into possession of the estate without any estimate of its value being recorded.

# CHAPTER IV

# DAYS OF DECLINE

He was then starting upon the downward course which was leading him to utter ruin. In the course of the following years, Fashion, who had decreed that he was the one painter to patronise, shook her fickle wings and flew off to others, and thenceforth decried her former favourite with the more ignorant dispraise because of her equally ignorant pæans in the past.

It was in vain that the Stathouder continued his patronage, giving him a commission for two pictures, "The Circumcision" and "The Adoration of the Shepherds," for which, on the twenty-ninth of September 1646, he paid the sum of 2400 florins, just double what he had paid before. It was in vain that the rising artists could not fail to perceive his transcendent merits, and that pupils from all Europe sought him out, Michiel Willemans, Ulric Mayr, and Franz Wulfhagen, Christoph Paudiss, Juriaen Avens, Bernard Keilh, Cornelis Drost, Nicholas Maes, Carel Fabritius, Samuel van Hoogstraten, and many more. He had ceased, apparently, to attract the public. At any rate, though his productive energy was unabated, his affairs grew ever more and more involved.

In 1647, Saskia's relations began to be alarmed, demanding

that the valuation of the property at the date of her death should be ascertained without delay, and Rembrandt replied that to the best of his belief it had been 40,750 florins. It is a little difficult to understand what right they had to formulate this demand, since, according to the will, the property was virtually Rembrandt's own, unless he married again, and this, to all appearance, he had, at that time, no idea of doing, though rumours to the contrary may well have reached their ears. A certain Geertje Dircx, the widow of one Abraham Clæsz, who had been engaged, probably not long after Saskia's death, as nurse to the infant Titus, who was always delicate, came in time to hope that she might aspire to rank as his step-mother; on January 24th, 1648, she made her will, neglecting the relations we know her to have had and bequeathing everything she legally could to Titus. Within two years, however, on October 1st, 1649, she repudiated her will, gave Rembrandt warning, and brought against him the equivalent of an action for breach of promise of marriage, to which he replied by an affidavit denying that their relations had ever been other than those of master and servant. In fact, her pretensions seem to have been only the delusions of her disordered brain, for in the course of the next year, 1650, she had to be removed and placed in confinement in a madhouse at Gouda, for which Rembrandt advanced the expenses, and, needless to say, never got them back.

We have not, moreover, far to seek for a reason for her explosion of temper in 1649 if she really believed her master meant to marry her, for on that very same October 1st, in reference to some otherwise unimportant disturbances of the neighbourhood by a drunken man, we find a certain Hendrickje Stoffels, of Ransdorp, in Westphalia, giving evidence on Rembrandt's behalf. Of the subsequent relations between her and Rembrandt there can be, unfortunately, no doubt whatever. She was at that time three-and-twenty, and a pleasant-looking girl enough, as her portrait, now in the Louvre, makes clear, and that her devotion to Rembrandt was not at all events self-seeking, the

☆ 50

future made abundantly evident. As long as she lived, she remained attached to him, through evil fortune and ill-report, and, though there was too good reason for the step, she is generally believed to have never asked or expected him to "make an honest woman of her," as the phrase goes. To this belief, however, I hesitate to subscribe; indeed, I incline to the conviction that the description of her given in a lawsuit on October 27th, 1661, as his lawful wife, "huysfrouw," the very title he himself gave to Saskia, was strictly accurate. There is not, it must be admitted, another particle of direct evidence that it was so, though this in itself is not to be despised, but there are circumstances not a few that point in the same direction.

While the connection was irregular, and to begin with, at least, it undoubtedly was so, there was never any concealment or shamefacedness about the matter, nor do Rembrandt's friends, not even the respectable Burgomaster Six, seem to have looked askance upon it. It is true that in 1654 she was summoned, somewhat tardily, before the Consistory of her church, severely admonished, and forbidden to communicate. That, of course, was inevitable from their point of view, and only shows how absolutely open the arrangement was. How improbable it is then that in later years she should have deliberately perjured herself on the question when, if it were perjury, the evidence to convict her must have been overwhelming. There can, indeed, have been no doubt, long before this church summons, as to the relations between them, for in 1652 she gave birth to a child which did not, however, survive long, as we know that it was buried in the Zuiderkerk on August 15th.

In October 1654, a second daughter was born, and was christened on October 30th, Cornelia, in itself a somewhat significant circumstance. We cannot, I fear, claim any very subtle delicacy of taste for Rembrandt, it appertained not to his race or time; but it seems more than strange that he should have given to an illegitimate child the name which had been borne by his mother and by two luckless infants of the dead Saskia. Taking all these facts together, I venture to conjecture that we may still hope to hear some day of the discovery of proof that some time, probably between July when she was rebuked, and October when the child was baptised, Rembrandt, moved perhaps by the public disgrace of the girl once more about to become the mother of his child, was duly married to her.

Indeed, if he had not married someone, how came it that in 1665 Louis Crayers, the guardian of Titus, was able to establish, before the Grand Council, his claim on behalf of his ward against Rembrandt's estate, then in bankruptcy, for 20,375 florins, the half of the property at the time of Saskia's death three-and-twenty years before? Unless Rembrandt had married again Titus would appear to have had no shadow of a claim to principal or interest, yet the case was fought out to the bitter end, and it seems quite incredible that the creditors should have been ignorant of, or should have failed to produce, so important a piece of evidence in their favour. Since Titus' claim was allowed, it is obvious that Rembrandt must have remarried, and, if so, there can be no doubt that it was to the true and faithful Hendrickje.

I have, however, been led to anticipate too far in the attempt to make this reasoning clear, and must return to 1649, in which year Rembrandt took a second step on his road to bankruptcy by ceasing to pay either instalments of the sum remaining due for the house, or even the interest upon it. Indications of the approaching disaster now follow thick and fast. At some time between 1650 and 1652 the pearl necklace which appears in so many of the pictures was sold to Philips Koninck. In 1651, so wholly out of favour was Rembrandt's art deemed to be, that Jan de Baer, a young artist, on leaving the studio of Backer, under whom he had been studying, after hesitating for awhile as to whether he should turn to Rembrandt or Van Dyck for further instruction, chose the latter, because his style was most durable.

By 1653 Rembrandt seems to have finally abandoned himself to the current which was drifting him so rapidly to wreck. On January 29th he borrowed 4180 florins from Cornelis Witsen on the hopeless undertaking to repay it in a year, and three days later, on February 1st, his long-suffering landlord Thysz entered a claim for 8470 florins still owing to him. Rembrandt, with a sharpness due probably rather to his lawyer than to himself, demanded that the title-deeds should be delivered to him first. Then, on March 14th, he borrowed a further 4200 florins from Isaac van Heertsbeeck, also repayable in a year, and after trying, apparently in vain, through François de Koster, to recover some of the large sums of money that must have been owing to him, he obtained from Six yet another loan on the guarantee of Ludowyck van Ludick. With this temporary relief he in part paid off Thysz, but 1170 florins still remained to be paid, and for this amount the creditor obtained a mortgage on the house.

The end was now drawing near. One more effort, however, was made to avert the crash. A certain Dirck van Cattenburch, a collector of works of art, presuming that, in the state of Rembrandt's affairs, the large house in the Breestraat could only be an encumbrance to him, proposed to relieve him of it by a sufficiently curious arrangement. He was professedly to sell him another, doubtless a smaller one, for 4000 florins; but, in fact, he was to give Rembrandt the house and 1000 florins in cash. For the remaining 3000 florins Rembrandt was to deliver pictures and etchings of that value, and furthermore? to etch a portrait, in a style not less finished than that of Six, of Dirck's brother Otto, the secretary of Count Brederode of Vianen, which was to be considered the equivalent of 400 florins. How far this elaborate transaction was carried out is uncertain. Rembrandt obtained the 1000 florins, and handed over pictures and etchings of his own, or from his collection, valued by Abraham Francen and van Ludick at over 3000 florins, but we hear no more of the house or the portrait.

It was in vain that his friends seem to have developed a perfect mania for being etched or painted by him – Six and Tholinx, Deyman the doctor, the two Harings, father and son – neither loans nor earnings could for long stave off the evil day. As if ill-luck dogged the family, his brother Adriaen had so managed to misconduct the business of the mill that he and the sister Lysbeth were also on the verge of ruin, and Rembrandt, in the midst of his own troubles, had to come to their assistance. Small wonder, then, that the end was hastened. On May 17th, 1656, one Jan Verbout was appointed guardian to Titus in the place of Rembrandt, and on the same day, before the Chamber of Orphans, the unfortunate artist transferred his rights in the house to his son. Soon afterwards he was formally declared bankrupt, and on July 25th and the following day an inventory was made "of paintings, furniture, and domestic utensils connected with the failure of Rembrandt van Rijn, formerly living in the Breestraat near the lock of St Anthony." The inventory still exists, and is full of interest, giving, as it does, a complete description of every room in the house, from the pictures in the studio to the saucepans in the kitchen, but want of space forbids any extended extracts from it here.

The law seems to have moved slower in those days even than in these. Rembrandt continued for some time to dwell in the house, and, apart from the business worries, the little family appears to have been a united and contented one. How united we discover from the will that Titus made on October 20th, 1657, and rectified on November 22nd. By that time Rembrandt's utter incapacity for business was probably recognised even by himself, and all that Titus possessed was left to Hendrickje and her daughter Cornelia in trust for him. Nevertheless, as if to smooth over the slur upon his father's improvidence, he provided that Rembrandt might draw a certain share, on condition that he did not employ it to pay his debts, a most unlikely use, it is to be feared, for him to put it to, except, like Falstaff, "upon compulsion." The remainder was to go to Cornelia on her marriage or coming of age. The whole of the interest, in the event of Rembrandt's death, was to go to Hendrickje and Cornelia, and there are certain other arrangements of less importance concerning the disposal of the property on Cornelia's decease.

☆ 54

A month later the law at last gave forth its pronouncement, and the commissioners authorised Thomas Jacobsz Haring, an officer of the Court, to sell the effects of the bankrupt by auction. The worst had befallen; the home in which he had passed eighteen years, many of them happy, and all full of industry, was his no more. The little family was temporarily broken up. Rembrandt moved to the Crown Imperial Inn, kept by one Schumann in the Kalverstraat, which ran southwards from the Dam, a handsome and commodious house, which had at one time been the Municipal Orphanage, and was then the customary place for holding auctions. Whether Hendrickje, Titus, and Cornelia went with him we do not know. M. Michel concludes, from the fact that Rembrandt's daily expenses, included in the records of the case, were three or four florins, that they certainly did not; but if the already-mentioned provision of 125 florins a year was considered sufficient support for the crippled brother, more than eight times that amount might surely have sufficed for four people, two of whom were children.

On December 25th, the sale of Rembrandt's property began in the very house where he was lodging, but only a small portion of the goods was then sold.

The wheels of the law, once started, ground evenly and small. On January 30th, 1658, the commissioners ordered the repayment to Witsen and van Heertsbeeck of the money they had lent. The heirs of Christoffel Thysz were also paid, in spite of the protests of Louis Crayers, who had by then replaced Verbout as guardian of Titus, and, as such, asserted his prior claim on the estate to the extent, according to Rembrandt's own estimate in 1647, 20,375 florins. The other creditors, taking advantage of Rembrandt's afore-mentioned failure to make an inventory at the time, protested loudly that the demand was much exaggerated, and a cloud of witnesses was summoned to give such evidence as they could concerning the possessions of the pair at the time that Saskia died. Several of these statements have already been referred to in this narrative; but, in addition, Jan Pietersz, a draper, Abraham

Wilmerdonx, director of the East India Company, Hendrick van Uylenborch, Nicholas van Cunysbergen, and others, gave testimony as to property owned by, or prices paid to, the bankrupt in former years.

In the meantime, on February 1st, 1658, at the request of Henricus Torquinius, the official who had charge of the business, the house in the Breestraat was sold to one Pieter Wiebrantsz, a mason, for 13,600 florins, but for some reason the bargain was not completed, and a second purchaser came forward with an offer of 12,000. There appear, however, to have been doubts as to his ability to pay, and it was finally transferred to a shoemaker, Lieven Simonsz, for 11,218 florins. Finally, in September, the pictures, engravings, and other objects of art were sold by auction, bringing in the ridiculous sum of 5000 florins, and all the possessions that Rembrandt had collected with such loving care and at so great a cost were scattered to the four winds.

It is pleasant to find that, in all this tribulation, many of his old friends still stood by him and endeavoured to help him to commissions. In 1660, for example, Govert Flinck, who was engaged on the decoration of the Grand Gallery in the Town Hall, having died, it became necessary to find someone to take his place. Rembrandt had never been much in favour with the town authorities, but on this occasion, possibly through the efforts of his old friend Tulp, who had been treasurer in 1658 and 1659, he was invited to carry on the work, and, as M. Michel has conclusively shown, painted for them a large picture of the conspiracy of Claudius Civilis. The opposition, however, apparently proved too strong, for it seems doubtful if the picture was ever seen in the place it was intended for. It did not, at any rate, remain there long.

On May 5th, 1660, we get another glimpse of the law proceedings when Heertsbeeck was ordered to pay back the 4200 florins which the Court had formerly awarded him, though Witsen was allowed to retain his 4180. On December 15th of the same year Hendrickje made a final effort to restore to some extent the prosperity of the household. With all proper circumstance, she entered on that day into partnership with Titus, legalising an association between them, informally established two years before, for the purpose of dealing in pictures, engravings, and curiosities. Both he and she contributed everything that they possessed to a common fund, and each was to be entitled to a half share of the stock. Rembrandt, partly, no doubt, from his proved incompetency for business, partly, perhaps, to keep out of the clutches of the creditors, was allowed no share whatever in the profits. As, however, it was necessary that Hendrickje, who knew nothing of such matters, and Titus, who was not yet of age, should have aid and assistance in the venture, and as no one was more capable of giving this than Rembrandt, it was provided that he should make himself as useful as possible in furthering the interests of the firm, and in return should have board, lodging, and certain allowances.

It was, perhaps, as judicious an arrangement as could be made for Rembrandt's sake, but it is not wonderful that the creditors, who saw all chances of their getting anything further vanishing into thin air, should have been fierce in their protests. How far the association prospered we do not know. Probably not too well, for Dr Bredius has gathered together a mass of evidence to show that a large proportion of the art-dealers in Amsterdam at that period came to disastrous financial ends. It served, at any rate, to keep a roof over their heads, and the wolf from the door, for we find them again settled down, this time in the Rozengracht, in a house opposite a pleasure garden called the Doolhof.

In 1661, an old friend again came to his support; for it was probably van de Cappelle, who was a dyer as well as a painter, who procured for him the commission to paint "The Syndics of the Drapers' Guild," which he so splendidly achieved. By this time there is some reason for supposing that yet another trouble was coming upon Rembrandt. As far as we know, he never executed any etchings after 1661, and M. Michel suspected that this might have been due to failing sight. A study, moreover, of the portraits painted from that time onwards, reveals the fact that a large majority of them, if not actually all, were conspicuously, some even enormously, larger than life, and that would in all probability be a symptom of the same misfortune. These two facts cannot, of course, be considered as furnishing absolute proof, but they certainly go to create a probability; nor can we regard the supposition that the overstrained nerves were giving way at last as in any way unlikely when we reflect how incessantly Rembrandt had worked his eyesight, and how minutely finished had been much of his work, especially among the etchings, many of which were undoubtedly executed by artificial light, after his day's painting was ended. It would be but one more burden of distress laid upon those heavily-laden shoulders.

In truth, the story of the few remaining years is but a record of stroke after stroke. On August 7th, 1661, the faithful Hendrickje was so seriously ill, that, in spite of its being a Sunday, she made her will, leaving, as was but right, all her property to Cornelia, but with the stipulation that, in case of her death, Titus was to inherit, though his father was to enjoy the income as long as he lived. That she recovered at that time we know from her appearance on October 27th, as a witness in the case of the drunken man already referred to; but the recovery must have been only temporary, for, after this last appearance, we hear of her no more, though we do not know the exact date of her death. There is, however, M. Michel believes, a reason for supposing it to have occurred in the autumn of 1662. On October 27th in that year Rembrandt sold the vault he had purchased in the Oudekerk, which was no longer his parish church. It was, nevertheless, an odd thing to do, since poor little Saskia lay there; and M. Michel, in seeking an explanation, conjectures that he was at that time under the necessity of providing for the burial of Hendrickje in the Westerkerk, and that the sale was a sheer necessity. There is, at any rate, no portrait of her known to have been painted after 1662, and the conjecture that she died that year is at least a plausible one.

In the course of the same year, we hear of the last pupil coming to Rembrandt, Aert de Gelder, whose youthful enthusiasm may have brought some brightness, we may hope, into the life of the poor broken old man. Meanwhile, the echoes of the law courts still rumbled in his ears, for, on December 22nd, Isaac Van Heertsbeeck, who had evidently not complied with the previous order of the Court in 1660, was again commanded to refund the 4200 florins, and again appealed.

Rembrandt had by then so completely dropped out of public ken, that we only get dim and fleeting glimpses of him. In 1664, we hear of him moving to the Lauriergracht, still farther to the south-east, and it is not until affairs draw him from seclusion that we learn more of him, and then only indirectly. We may, perhaps, conclude, however, from the scarcity of his works during these last years, that his eyes, and possibly general health, were getting ever worse.

On January 27th, 1665, van Heertsbeeck's protracted struggle came to an end, and the Grand Council decided that by June 20th the money must be repaid. On June 19th, Rembrandt and Titus appealed to the law to anticipate the coming of age of the latter, so that he might be legally considered of years of discretion before the actual arrival of his twenty-fifth birthday, a request which must have been connected with a foreknowledge of the decision delivered the next day, June 20th, in favour of Louis Crayers. This meant that the rights of Titus to the full amount of his mother's fortune of 20,375 florins were allowed; but only 6952 florins remained, and of this, on November 5th, Titus was authorised to take possession in his own name. It was but a scanty fraction of what he should have had, but it was something, and the little windfall may have had some part in the return of the family to the Rozengracht. Of the next two years we know nothing, except that we learn from a portrait of Jeremias de Decker, a poet who wrote eulogistic verses on the painter, that neither the man nor the artist was entirely neglected. The first sounds that come again to us out of the darkness are those of wedding bells on the occasion of the marriage of Titus with his cousin Magdalena, the daughter of Cornelia van Uylenborch and of Albert van Loo, whose quarrel with Rembrandt years before had clearly been forgotten. The note of merriment was, however, too quickly changed for one of dolour, for ere the year was out Titus was dead, as we learn from the record of his burial in the Westerkerk, on September 4th, 1668.

In March 1669, the widowed Magdalena gave birth to a daughter, and, on the twenty-second of that month, Rembrandt stood by while the only grandchild he was to see was christened Titia. We catch thereafter some murmurs of that business which he so hated, in connection with the settlement of the respective shares which the little Titia and Cornelia were to draw from the remainder of the old association between their respective parents; and then again comes silence, until, from an entry in the Doelboek, the registry of deaths in the Westerkerk, we learn that the long, slow, downward path has ended, where all paths end, in the grave.

"Tuesday, 8 October, 1669, Rembrandt van Rijn, painter, on the Rozengracht, opposite the Doolhof. Leaves two children."

He was buried, at the cost of thirteen florins, at the foot of a staircase leading up to a pulpit on a pillar on the left-hand side as you go up the church; but when, some years back, a coffin, supposed to have been his, was opened, not a trace of his ashes was to be found.

The subsequent history of the family may be briefly sketched. Within a fortnight of Rembrandt's death, on October 13th, his daughter-in-law Magdalena was also dead. On the 16th and 18th of March, and again on April 15th, Abraham Francen, the old and faithful friend, and Christian Dusart, acting on behalf of Cornelia, settled with François van Bylert, acting on behalf of the baby Titia, their respective portions of the small inheritance. François would seem to have been a kindly guardian, and Titia to have had a happy home, for, on June 16th, 1686, at the church of Slooten, she married his son, also named François, a jeweller, living in the Kloveniers-Burgwal, in the heart of her native town. Here she bore, and buried also in the Westerkirk, three children, one in 1688, one in 1695, and one in 1698, and herself died November 22nd, 1725, leaving a fourth child, who only survived her three years.

Cornelia married a man named Suythoff, and with him travelled to Java, where, in the town of Batavia, she gave birth to two sons, one on December 5th, 1673, called Rembrandt, the other, on July 14th, 1678, named Hendrick.

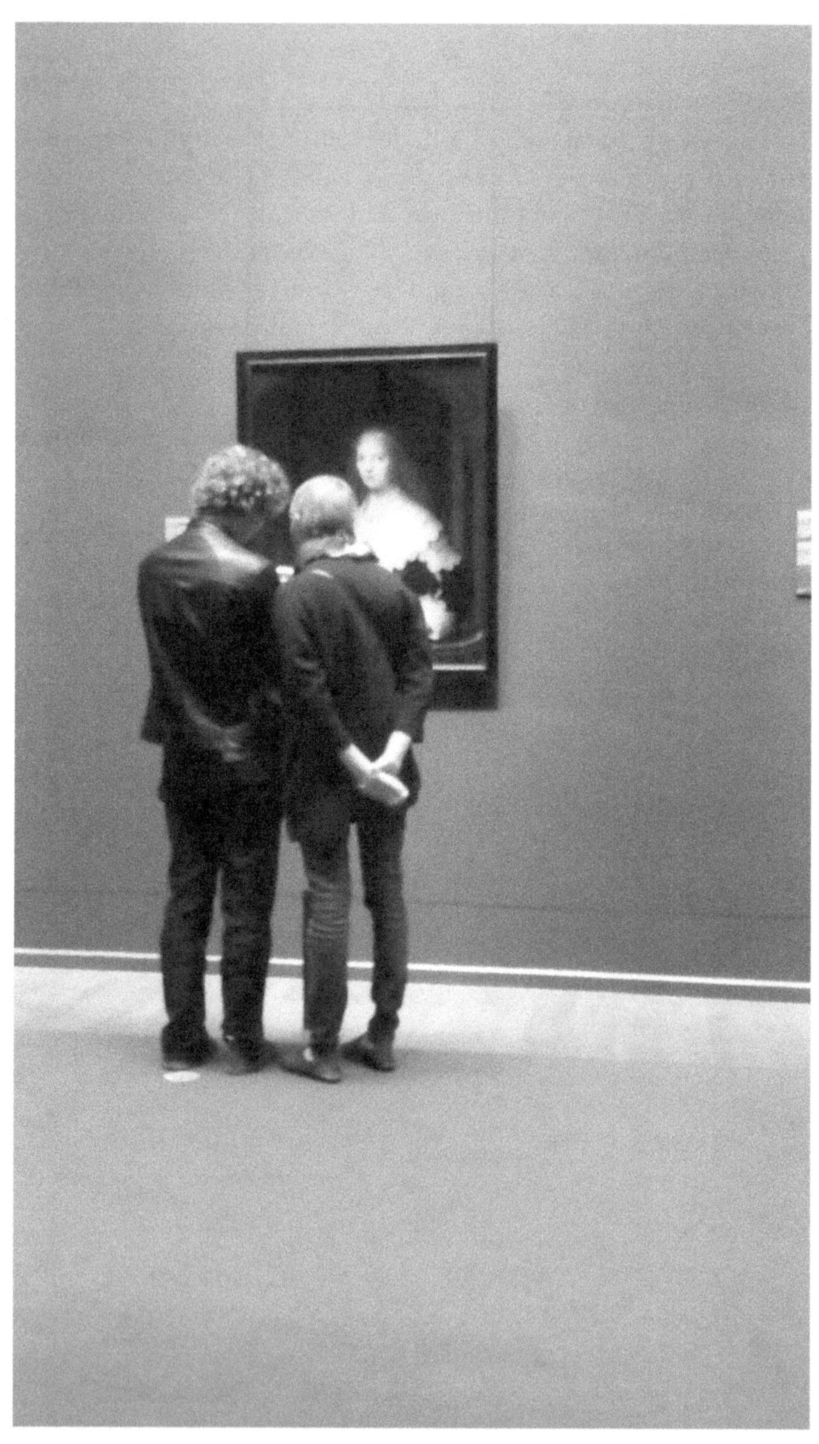

Rembrandt in the Rijksmusem, Amsterdam, 2015
(this page and over. Photos: J. Robinson).

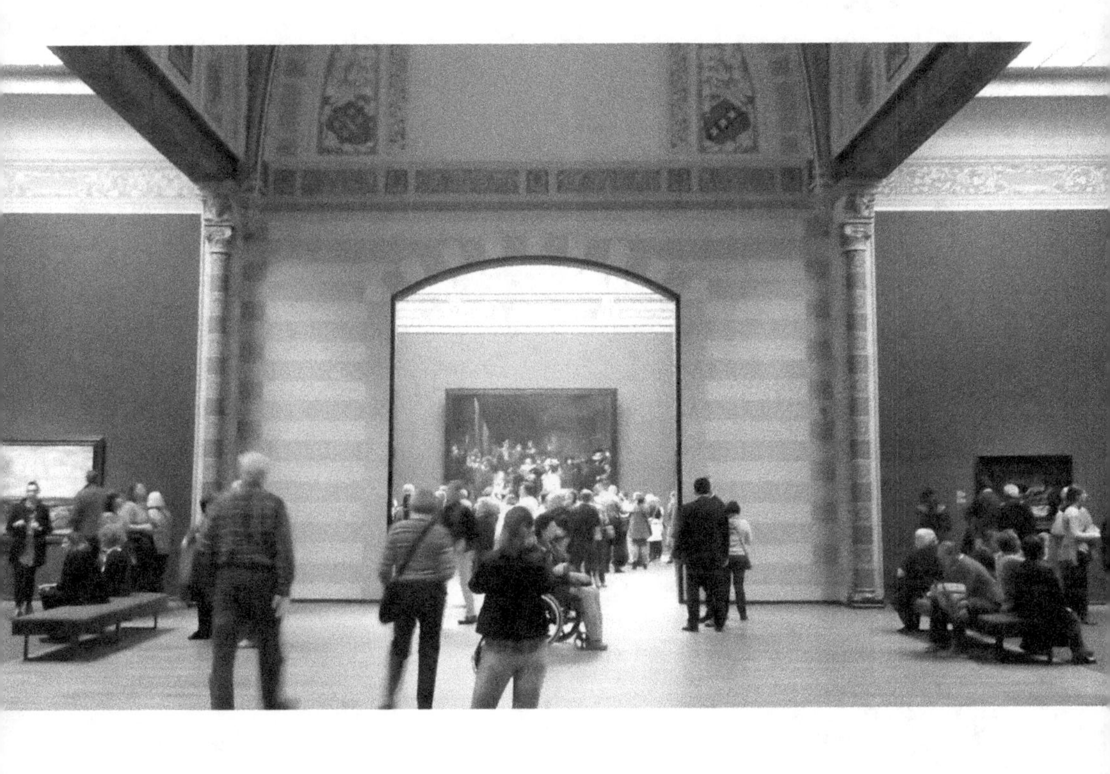

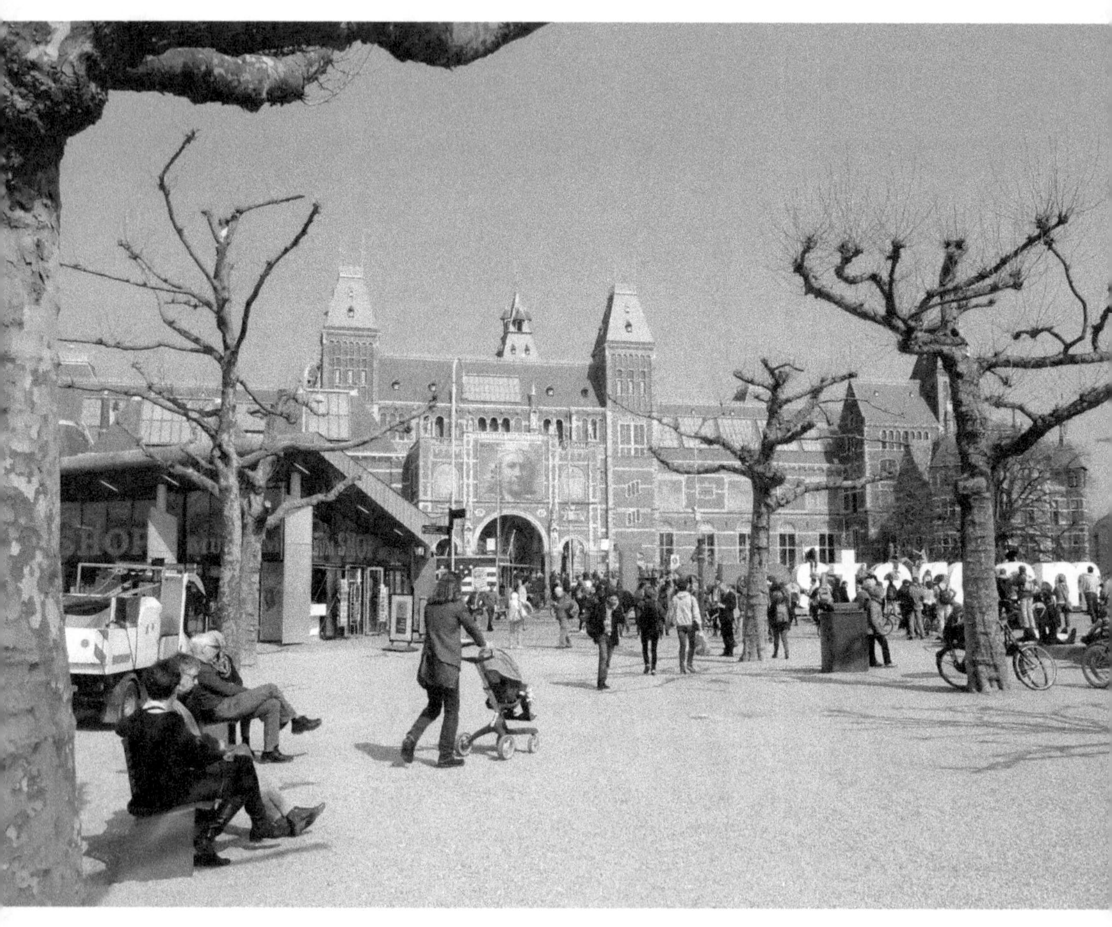

The Rijksmuseum in Amsterdam

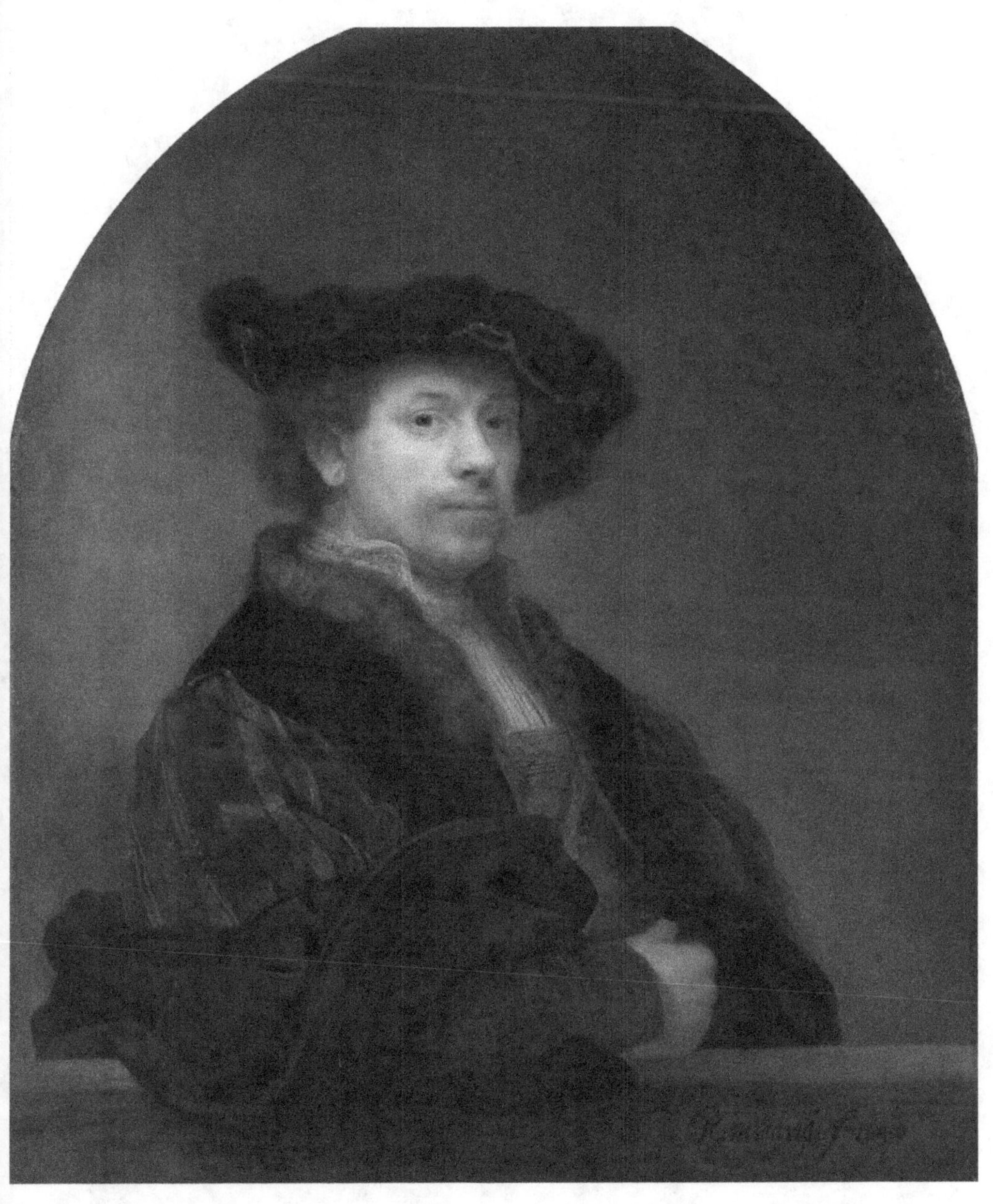

Rembrandt, Self-Portrait, 1640, London
(this page and over)

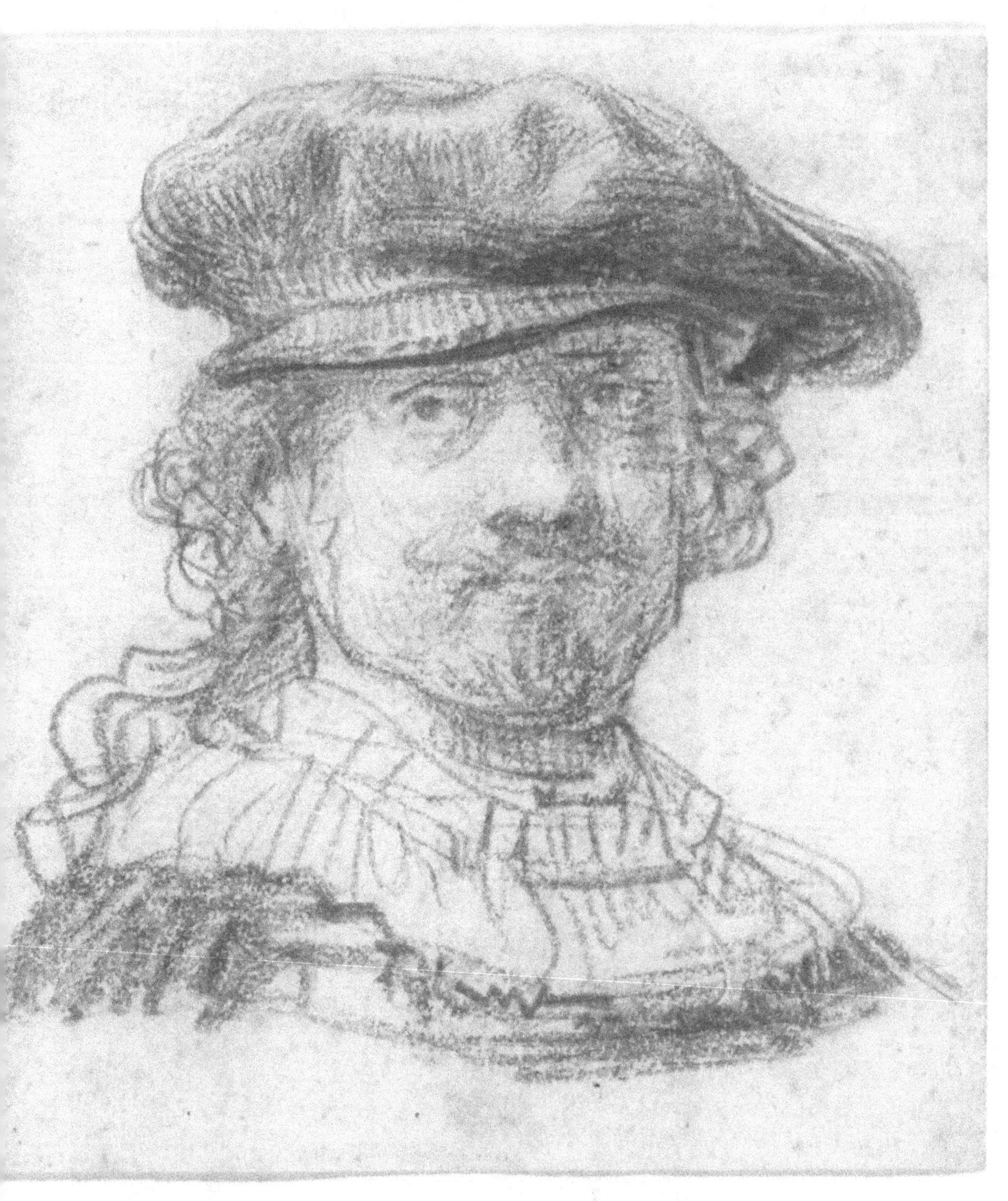

Rembrandt van Rijn, Self-Portrait, c.1637, Washington, DC

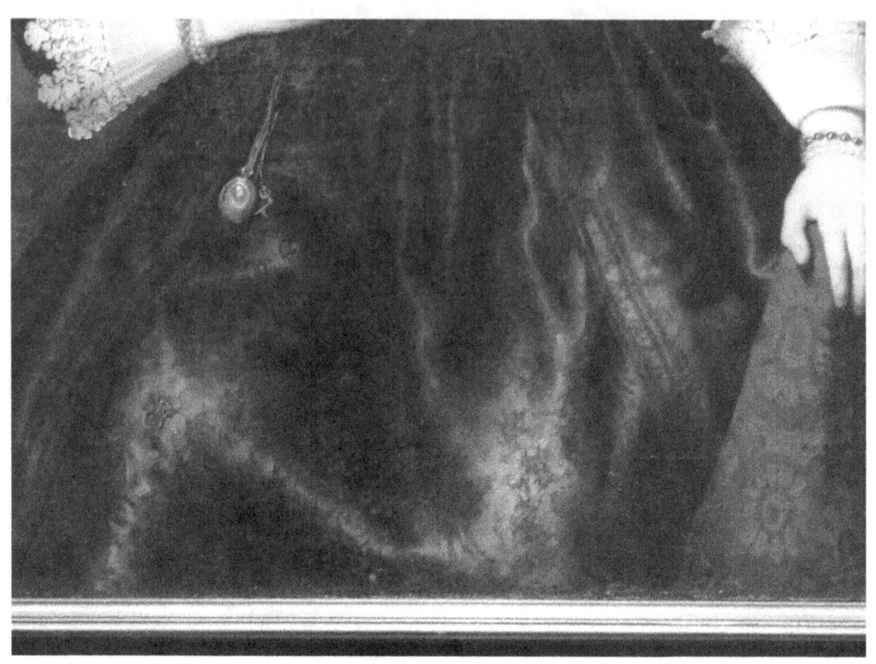

Rembrandt, Portrait of a Young Woman, details

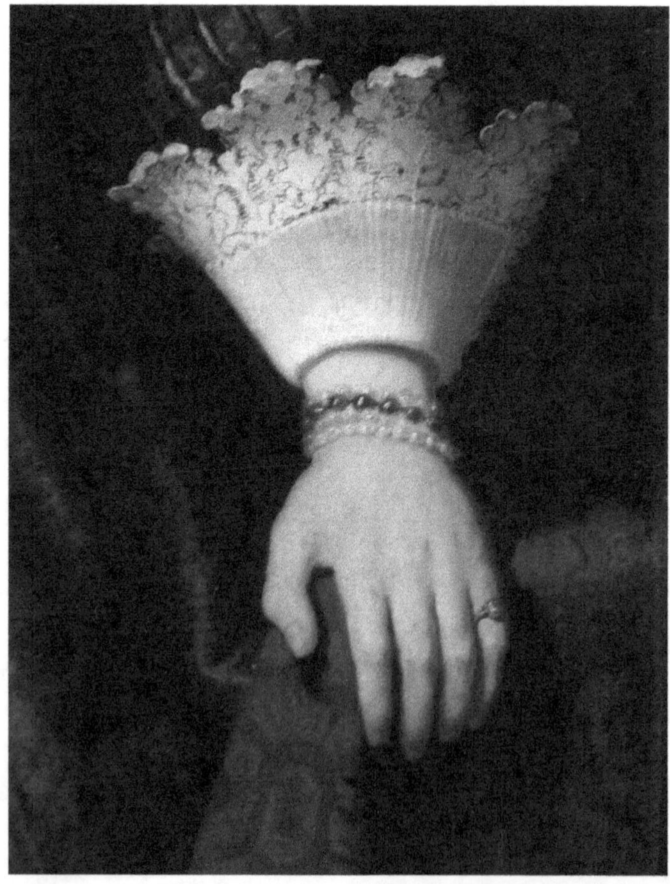

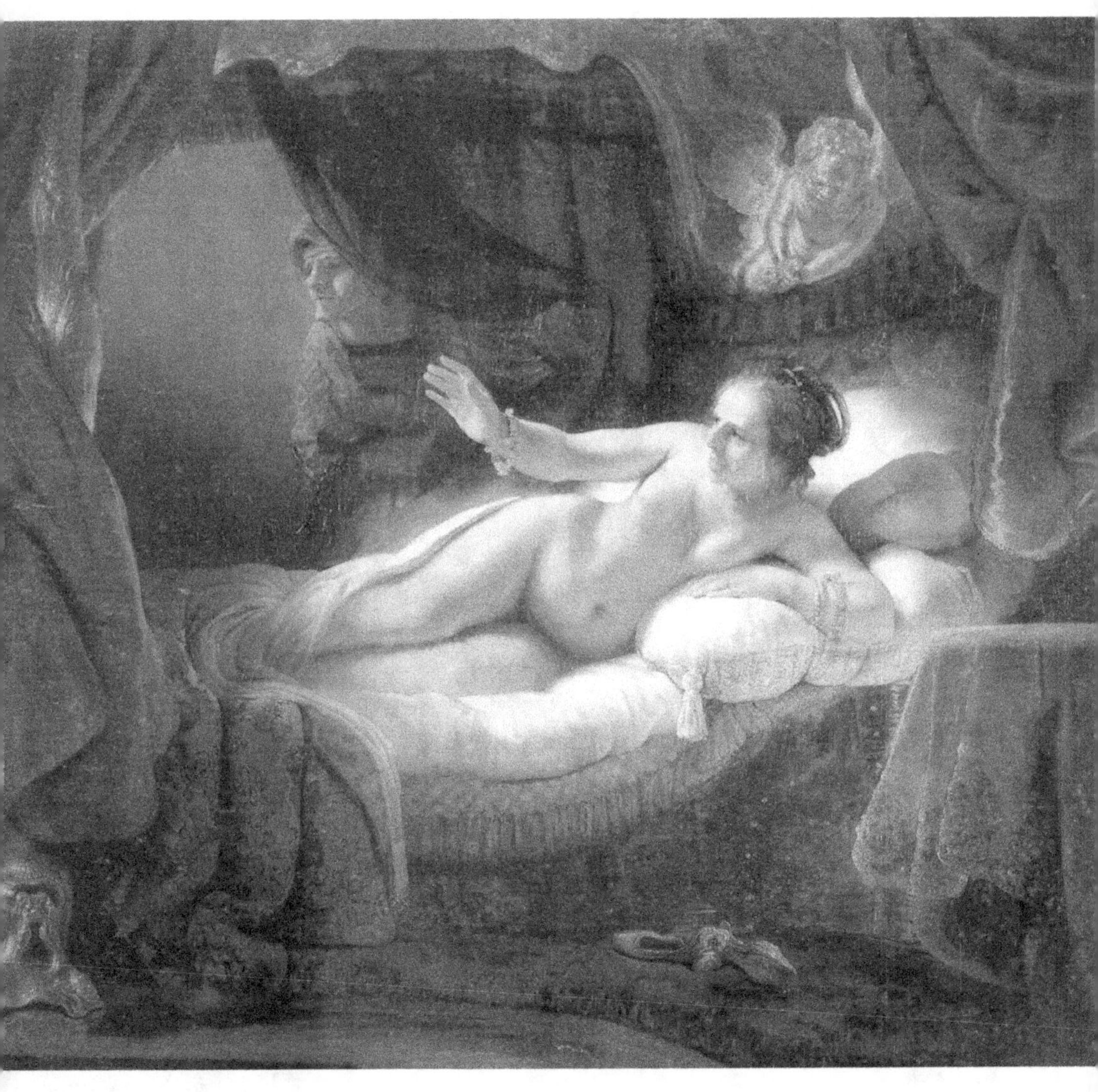

Rembrandt van Rijn, Danae, 1636, St Petersburg

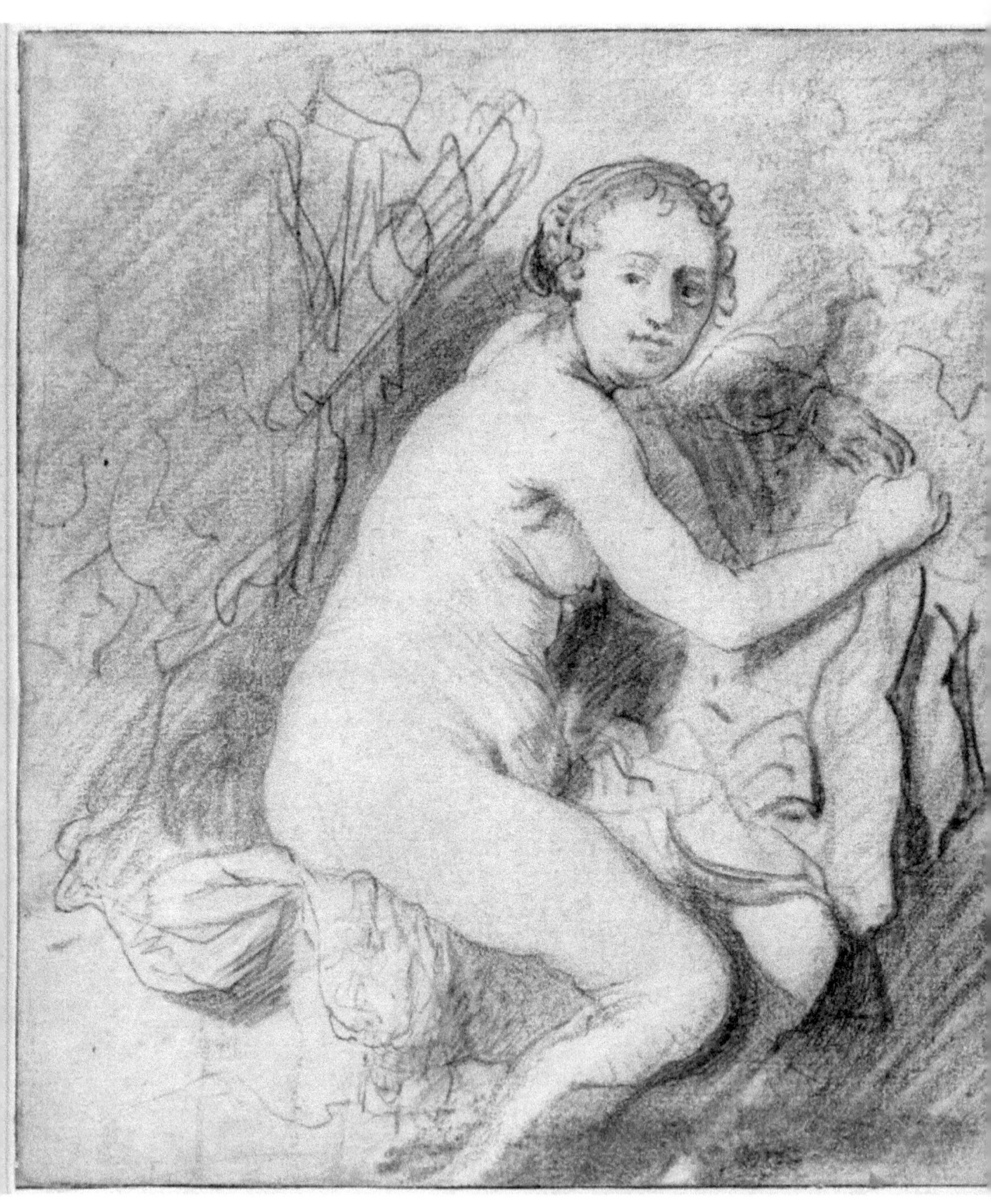

Rembrandt van Rijn, Diana At the Bath, 1630-31, British Museum

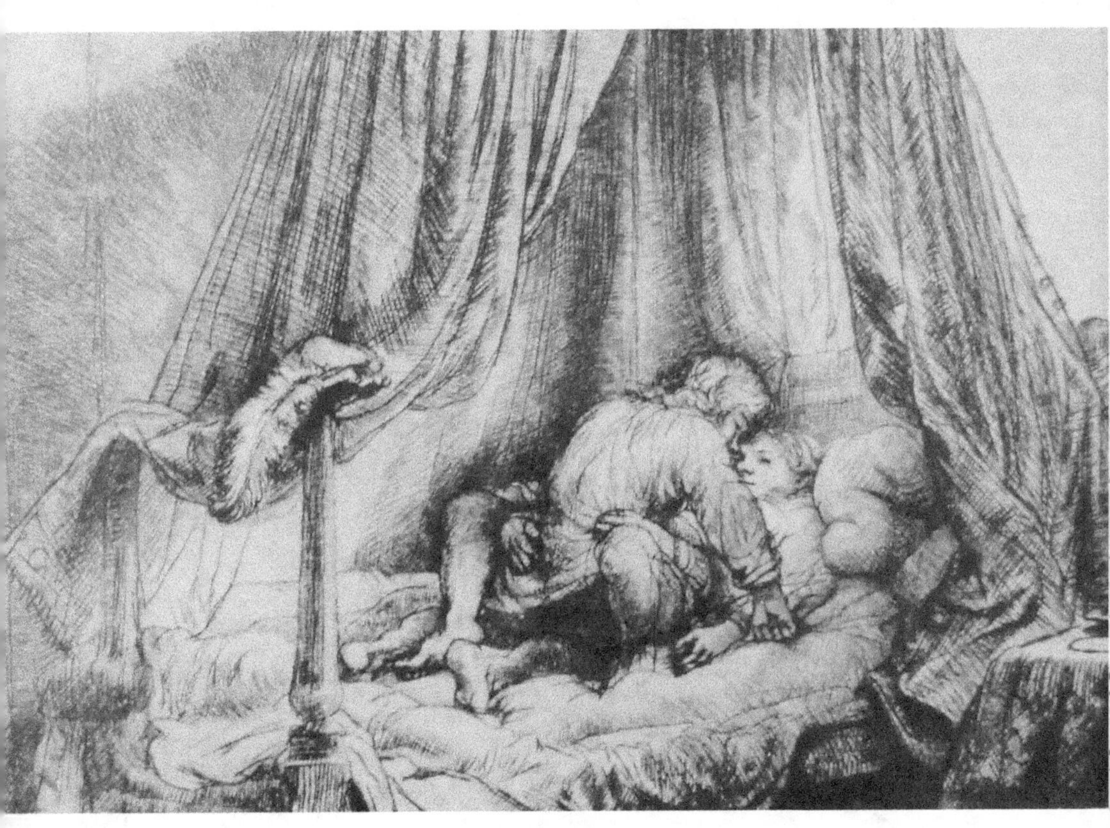

Rembrandt van Rijn, Ledakant, 1646

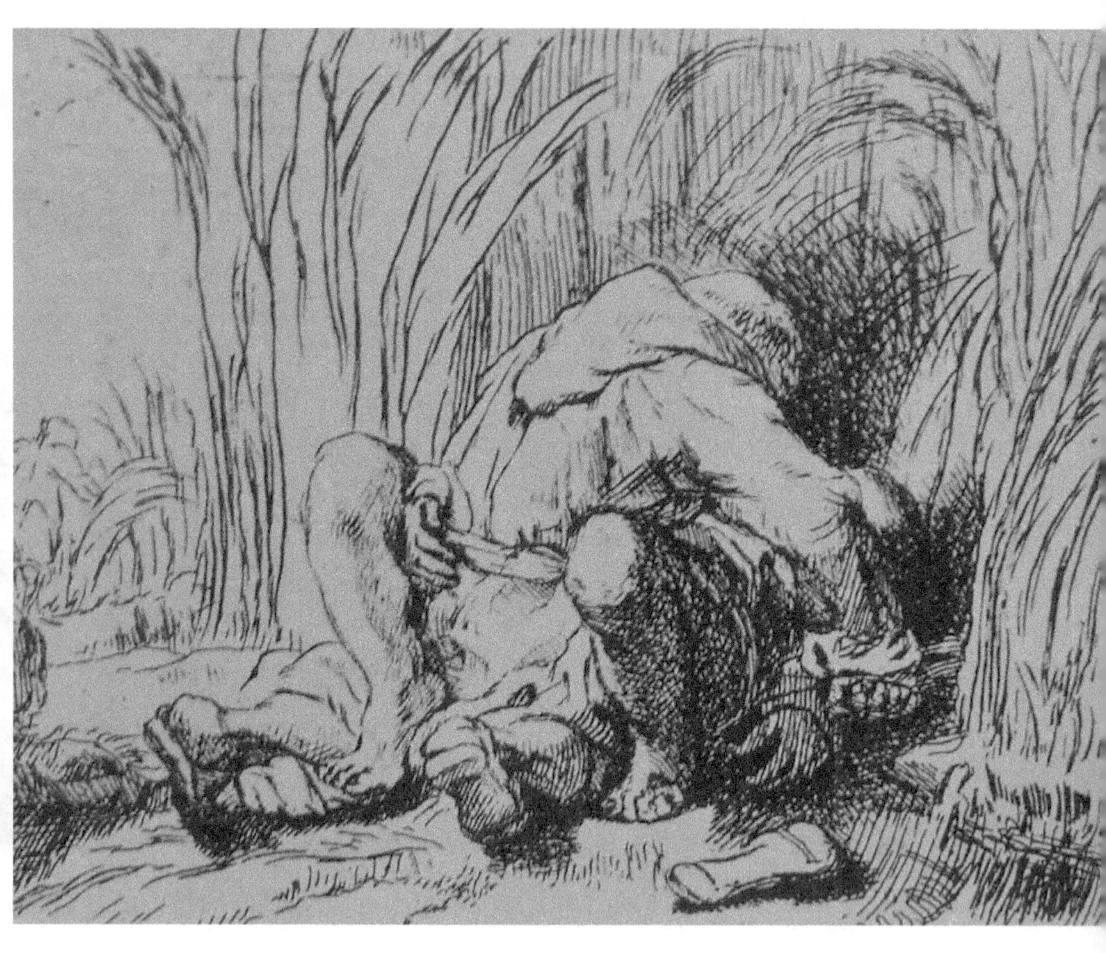

Rembrandt van Rijn, The Monk In the Cornfield

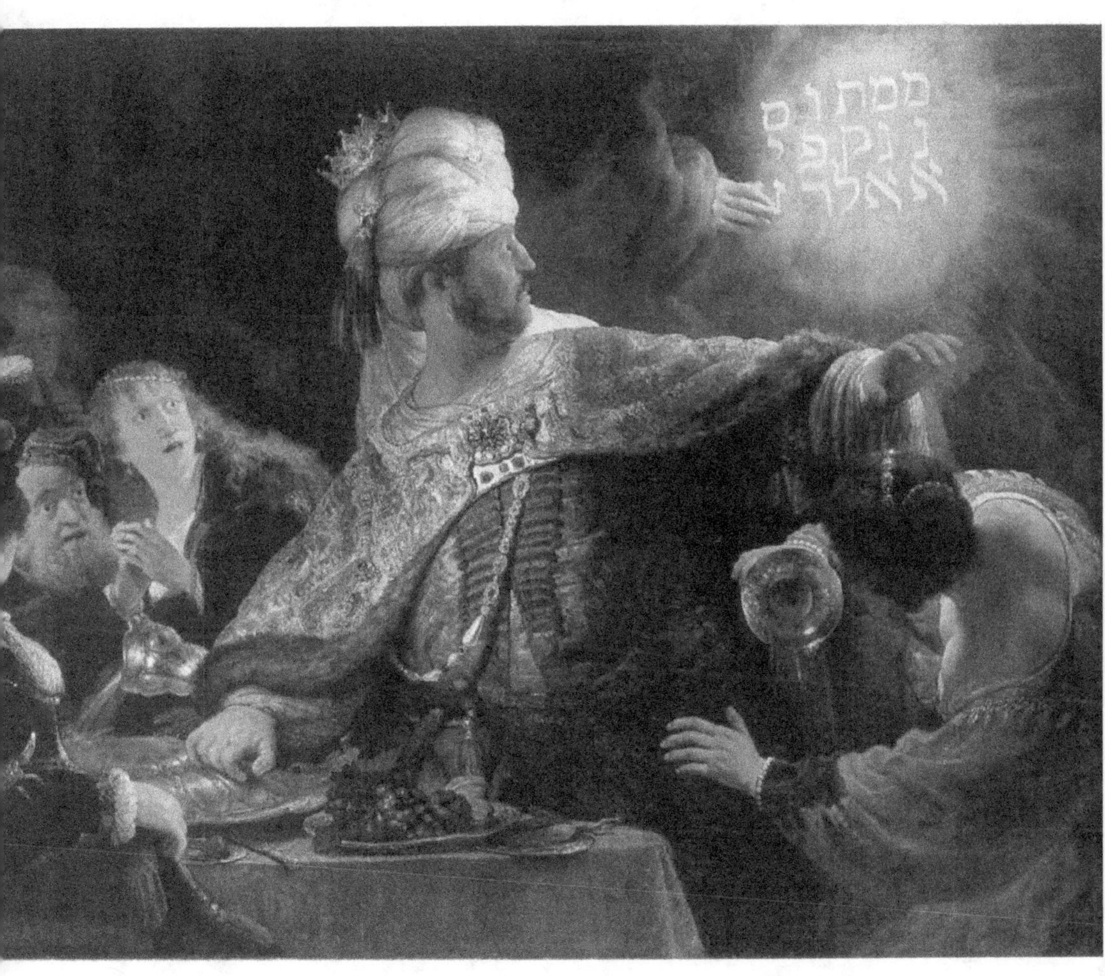


Rembrandt van Rijn, Belshazzar's Feast, 1635, National Gallery, London

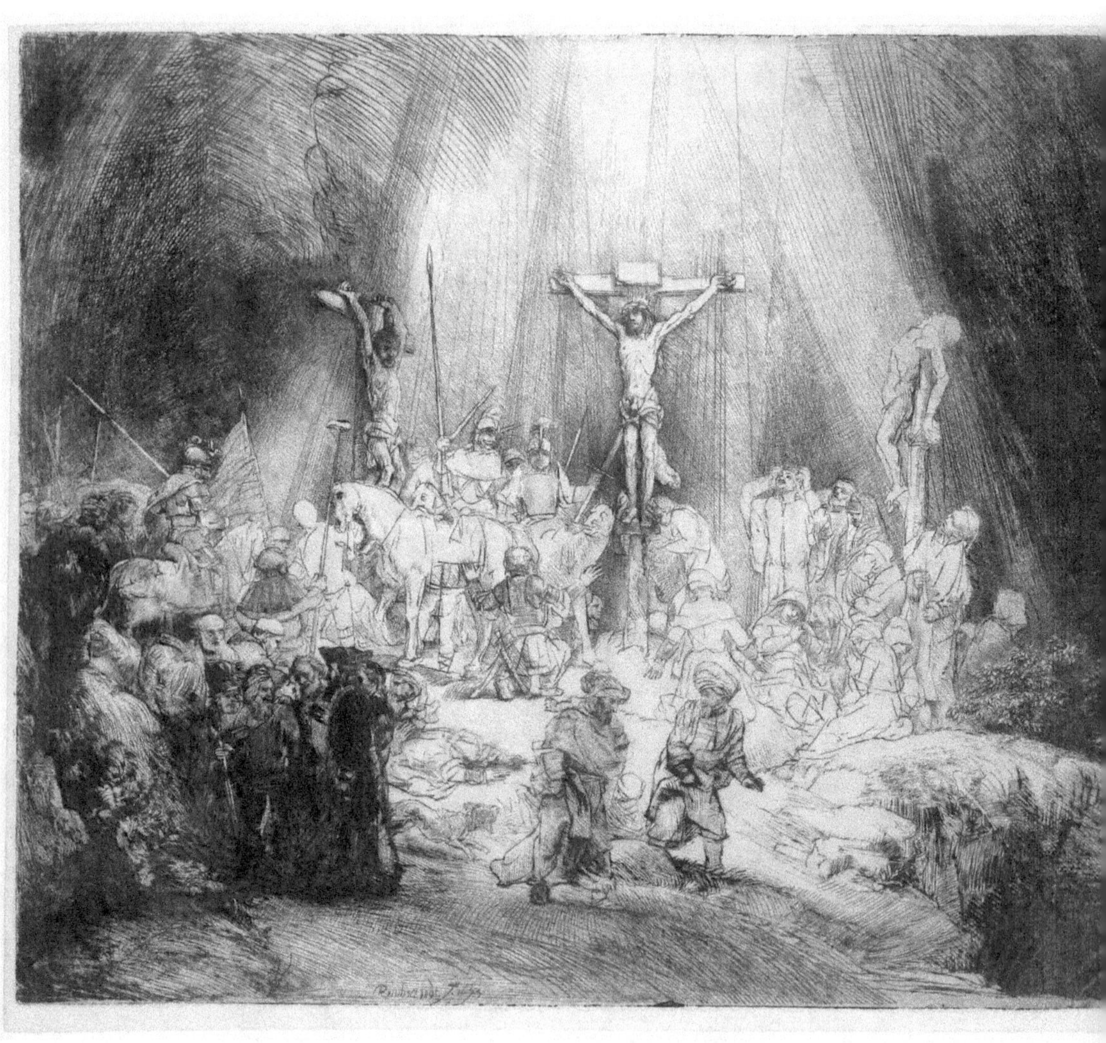

Rembrandt, The Three Crosses, 1653

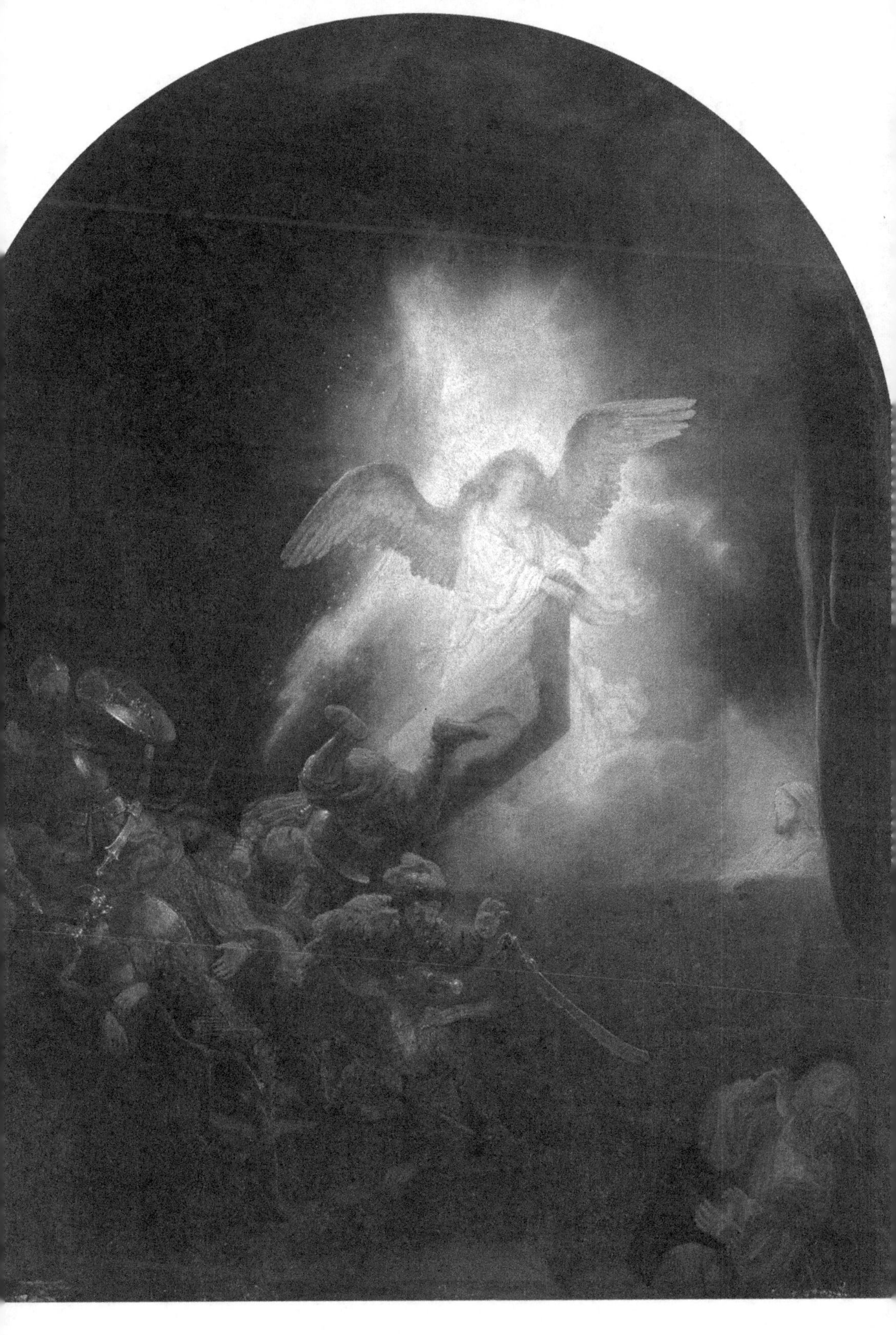

Rembrandt, The Resurrection

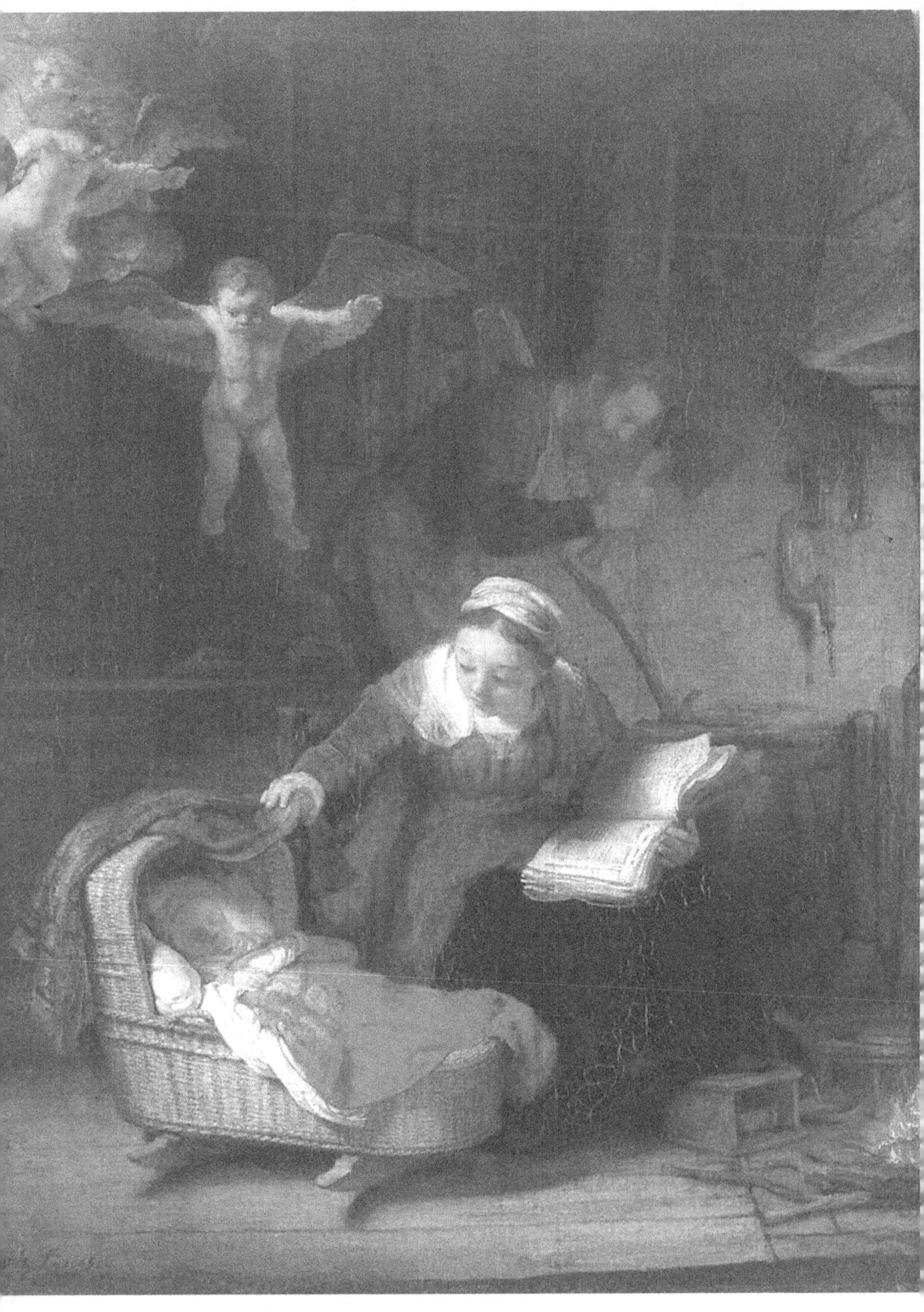

Rembrandt van Rijn, The Holy Family With Angels, 1645, Hermitage Museum

# PART II

# REMBRANDT THE PAINTER

# CHAPTER V

# EARLY YEARS (1627-1633)

Of the blank spaces in the record of Rembrandt's career, none is so long or so inexplicable as that which begins with his return from Amsterdam to Leyden in 1624. Here the track breaks off abruptly, and we can be sure of nothing until we come to the first known pictures signed by him, and dated 1627.

We will take first the picture discovered by Sir J. C. Robinson about twenty years ago, and presented by him to the Berlin Gallery. It represents a wrinkled old man, seated at a table. Papers and account books lie around him, and are heaped up in the background, and on his left, resting on a thick volume, stands a fat purse. A pair of scales are in front of him, and beside them a dozen or so of coins. Lifting a candle in his left hand, he throws the light of it upon a piece of money. The work, though promising, is in no way startling, and he would have been an acute critic who could have foretold from it the lofty height to which the painter of it was to soar. It is signed, with one of the ever-varying forms of his signature, R.H., combined in a monogram, followed by the date 1627.

The other picture known to belong to this first year, "St Paul in Prison," is in the Museum at Stuttgart [No. 225], and presents much the same merits of close observation, much the same defects of timid execution as the last. It represents the saint seated in a straw-strewn dungeon, lighted by a single beam of sunlight, surrounded by books, with the sword that symbolises him, meditating before writing. The signature in this case is a double one: the first, consisting of his full name, with one of his curious mis-spellings, Rembrand, and underneath fecit; the second an elaborate R followed by f. 1627, and below the down stroke, crossing the tail of the R, a smaller L, which Dr Bode suggests stands for Leydensis.

Three other pictures, all undated, are attributed to this year or the next, a "Philosopher reading by Candle-light," painted on copper, "A Study of Himself," at Cassel [No. 208], and a "Portrait of his Mother," which was lent for a time to the Ryksmuseum at Amsterdam, but is there no longer.

In the Cassel picture, small as it is, the breadth and vigour of treatment, the courage of the work are so remarkable that it is difficult to believe that it is of the same period as the previous pictures. It is a study of little more than the head, presenting one of those effects of contrasted light and shade which he so loved that pseudo-art slang has nicknamed them of late years Rembrandt effects. The shadows are a little dark, the contrasts are a little forced, wanting the true gradations, but the power displayed is so great, the frankness of the handling so certain that, especially in a photograph, the little study has all the appearance of a life-sized picture.

There are again two pictures dated in the following year, 1628. "Samson captured by the Philistines," at Berlin, is a not too successful first attempt at a composition of several figures, but it is of interest to the student as showing the sternly practical bent of Rembrandt's imagination, the intense craving for a strictly probable conception of the scene which, though at times it led him over the border of the simple into the absolutely ludicrous, more often gives that wonderfully impressive vitality and depth of feeling to his pictures. Here, as elsewhere, he aims not at all at heroic attitudes and over-dramatic effect; he makes no attempt to invent the scene as it ought to have looked, but endeavours to realise how it did look. The Philistines, he knew, were afraid of Samson, and he will not bate a jot of their terrors. One of them advances in fear and trembling, carefully keeping Delilah between himself and the object of his dread; while the other hides unequivocally behind the bed-curtains.

Here, also, we find an instance of his habit of painting in accessories because they were picturesque and available, quite regardless of their appropriateness, in the Malay kriss thrust into Samson's belt; and here we find for the first time that blending of the features of the two earlier monograms, the R.H. of the one, with the L. of the other, into the thenceforth frequent combination R.H.L. with the date 1628.

The second picture, bearing the same monogram and date, is in the possession of Herr Karl von der Heydt of Elberfeld, showing a man in full armour, standing by a fire in a courtyard, and closely observed by soldiers and servants, which Dr Bode not unreasonably believes to represent "The Denial of St Peter." Seven other pictures are attributed to about that date, one of which is believed by its possessor, Dr Bredius, to be a "Portrait of Rembrandt's Mother". There are also a copy of this, showing a little more of the figure, attributed to Rembrandt, but probably by another hand; two portraits supposed to be "The Painter's Father," one lent by Dr Bredius to the Museum at the Hague [No. 565], the other in the Museum at Nantes; a "Portrait of a Boy," at Hinton St George, and a doubtful one of "A Young Girl," called Rembrandt's sister Lysbeth, at Stockholm [No. 591]. A "Judas with the Price of the Betrayal," in the collection of Baron Arthur de Schickler of Paris, is considered by M. Michel to be the identical picture to which Constantin Huygens referred in that eulogy which has been mentioned in the painter's life. A "Raising of Lazurus," in the collection of Mr Yerkes in New York, completes the list.

There is only one picture bearing the date 1629, a small "Portrait of Himself," at Gotha [No. 181]; but there are eleven others believed to have been painted about that time. Two are in the Mauritshuis at the Hague. A "Bust of Himself" [No. 148] is a strong, resolute piece of work, and a marked advance on all that he had done before. The other picture at the Hague [No. 598] is supposed to be his elder brother Adriaen. There is less doubt about a portrait in the Ryksmuseum at Amsterdam [No. 1248], painted about that time, though bearing a forged signature and the impossible date 1641. It is that of a man with a short peaked beard and grey moustaches martially brushed up, and a long aquiline nose. The same features occur frequently in the earlier pictures and etchings, and M. Michel has made out a very good case for their being those of Harmen Gerritsz, the painter's father.

There are three other "Portraits of Himself," "A Head of a Boy," "A Young Man Laughing," and a "St Peter," all painted about that time; but of more importance are two small subject-pictures. The first, signed R.H., but not dated, "Christ at Emmaus," in the possession of Madame André-Jacquemart of Paris, is the earliest example of that presentment of a group of figures lighted by artificial light, to which Rembrandt was so partial. Here, as in most cases, the source of the light is hidden, as it stands on a table, on the right of the picture, in front of which Christ is seated, in profile to the left, his silhouette sharply cut against the radiance. At his feet one of the disciples kneels. The second, seated in the centre, on the further side of the table, lifts up his hands in amazement. On the left, in the background, the secondary softer illumination, so frequently introduced in similar effects by Rembrandt, is provided by the glow of firelight on two women engaged in cooking. The other is "The Presentation in the Temple," in the collection of Consul Weber at Hamburg. Like the last, it is signed, with the full name Rembrandt however, but is not dated, and the effect is to some extent marred by the harshness of the contrasts of light and shade, his later complete grasp of subtle transitions being still imperfectly developed.

Six out of the seventeen pictures attributed to 1630 or thereabouts are signed and dated, and one, a reproduction of the

"Portrait of his Father," in the Hermitage at St Petersburg [No. 814], is signed with the monogram R.H.L., but not dated; while a different portrait of the same, at Rotterdam [No. 237], is signed R. alone. Four of these are portraits: one, at Hamburg, of "Maurice Huygens," the brother of the painter's admirer Constantin; one, in the collection of Count Andrassy at Buda-Pesth, his own; one, at Cassel, of an unknown "Old Man" [No. 209]; and one, in the Ferdinandeum at Innsbruck, though called "Philon the Jew," is probably his father. One of the two subject-pictures, in the Six collection, Amsterdam, is a sketch, broadly but expressively handled, of "Joseph interpreting his Dreams," signed with the full name Rembrandt, 1630. The other, signed R.H.L. 1630, in the collection of Count Stroganoff, is of doubtful import. It represents an old man seated in a cave, resting his head upon his right hand, while his left rests on a large book. Beside him lie a cloth embroidered with gold, various gold vessels, and other objects of value. In the distance is seen a town in flames, from which the inhabitants are hurriedly escaping. What it is intended to represent is an unsolved riddle, and the title of "A Philosopher in Meditation," though convenient to identify it by, has not otherwise much significance. The remaining eleven pictures are studies or portraits, of which the old woman, belonging to the Earl of Pembroke, a bust of "A Young Girl," the property of Dr Bredius, and lent by him to the Hague Museum, and another "Portrait of an Old Woman" resembling somewhat in features the picture at Wilton, but known, for some mysterious reason as, "The Countess of Desmond," may be mentioned.

At what time in 1631 Rembrandt moved to Amsterdam we have no means of judging, nor can we say with any certainty which pictures of that year were painted before, which after, his change of residence. A "Bust of his Father," signed R.H.L. 1631, the property of Mr Fleischmann, was probably among the former. The "Young Man with the Turban," at Windsor, must also, presumably, have been painted before his removal, if M. Michel is justified in his belief that it is a portrait of Gerard Dou. Of the others we know nothing that points either way.

Rembrandt was now beginning to find himself. The dry precision, the timid carefulness have disappeared. His hand moves easily about its appointed task, not indeed, as yet, with the splendid freedom of later years, but with an assured confidence. He knows what he wants to do, and begins to feel that he can do it. The commissions that finally necessitated his establishment in Amsterdam showed him also, we may suppose, that other people appreciated the fact, and we may, perhaps, refer to this growing confidence in himself the great increase in the number of pictures signed that year. There are eleven, bearing both date and signature, two signed, but undated, and two which, though bearing neither date nor signature, are believed to have been painted about that time.

Of the first class, a picture of a man reading, in the Museum at Stockholm [No. 579], known as "St Anastasius," bears yet another version of the painter's name, the d being absent in this case, so that it reads Rembrant. A "Holy Family," at Munich [No. 234], signed Rembrandt, is an example of a propensity, which he never thoroughly shook off, to over-compose his pictures.

The same over-marked arrangement, though, to a far less degree, is also observable in the pyramidal group in the otherwise splendid "Presentation in the Temple," at the Hague [No. 145]. This is signed with the initials R.H. alone, interlaced, but seven others bear the three, R.H.L., including the portrait of Gerard Dou, already mentioned; a portrait, said to be his mother, at Oldenburg [No. 166], wearing a semi-oriental dress, and reading, from which circumstance the picture has obtained the name of "The Prophetess Anna"; and the "Portrait of a Merchant," long called "Coppenol," in the Hermitage at St Petersburg [No. 808].

Of the two undated pictures, "Zachariah receiving the Prophecy of the Birth of John the Baptist," in the collection of M. Albert Lehmann, Paris, bears the full name Rembrandt. The mysterious figure at Berlin [No. 828C.], a young woman in a rich dress, seated by a table, on which lie pieces of armour, a book, and a lute, while other arms, including a shield, decorated with a gorgon's head, hang on the wall above her, gaming for her the fanciful titles "Judith" or "Minerva," has only vague traces of the initial R. Of the last class, one is a copy, formerly in the Beresford-Hope collection, of the "Portrait of his Father," in the Ryksmuseum, the other is a small figure of "Diana Bathing," in the collection of M. Warneck, Paris.

Once satisfactorily established in Amsterdam, Rembrandt increased his annual production marvellously. The number of pictures known or believed to belong to each of the four preceding years, are, in succession, four, nine, twelve, and twenty, the numbers for the four succeeding years are, respectively, forty-two, thirty, twenty-six, and twenty-seven; or, taking the average of each period, we find that the first would give a little more than eleven pictures per annum, the second, very nearly thirty. 1632, in especial, when he was new to Amsterdam, was a year of extraordinary energy.

We find also, at the same time, a vast increase in the number of signed pictures, yet still note a surprising variety in the form the signature takes. No less than thirty are signed, and all but two of these are also dated. Nine of them bear the monogram, R.H.L., and ten others have the same, with, for the first time, the addition van Rijn, while one has the plain initial R. with van Rijn added. One, forming a sort of transition with the other group, is signed Rembrandt H.L. van Rijn, and nine are signed with the full name, in three of which the d is missing. Thirty-four of the pictures are portraits, and six of them form pairs representing husband and wife – namely, "Burgomaster Jan Pellicorne, with his son Caspar," and "Suzanna van Collen, his Wife, and her Daughter," in the Wallace collection; an unknown Man and his Wife, in the Imperial Museum, Vienna, though these four are only believed to belong to that year; the portraits of "Christian Paul van Beersteyn," and "Volkera Nicolai Knobbert," his wife, in the possession of Mr Havemeyer of New York, alone bearing the date. There is also a portrait at Brunswick [No. 232], fantastically called "Grotius," the companion of which was painted next year; another, believed, with good reason, to represent "Dr Tulp," formerly in the collection of the Princess de Sagan, which is also one of a pair, though the picture of the wife was not painted until two years later; and a third, in the collection of M. Pereire, Paris, of a man, whose wife was also not painted till the following year. Twelve others represent actually or conjecturally known individuals, but two of these, if, as is probable, they represent the painter's father, must have been painted earlier, as would also be the case with four others more doubtfully described, two as his mother, two as his sister. One at Cassel [No. 212] almost certainly represents "Coppenol, the Caligraphist," and an admirable picture in Captain Holford's collection, is undoubtedly "Martin Looten," a merchant of Amsterdam; while, even in that busy year, he found time once to paint his own portrait. The other four include the two of "Saskia," already mentioned in the Life, and two men, one said to be "Matthys Kalkoen," and one, a certain "Joris de Caulery."

So engaged was he on portraiture, that he only found time for three small figure subjects, if, indeed, they were painted that year, for none is dated. One, in the Wallace collection, is "The Good Samaritan"; the second at Berlin [No. 823], represents "Pluto in his Chariot carrying off Proserpine," quite the most successful of Rembrandt's rare appeals to classical mythology for inspiration; while the third at Frankfort [No. 183], is a somewhat indifferent rendering of "David playing the Harp before Saul."

I have left to the last, the great work of that year, the famous "Anatomy Lesson," at the Hague. In producing this, the largest and most ambitious work he had yet attempted, one, moreover, the success or failure of which could scarcely help having a marked influence on his future career, Rembrandt, we cannot but perceive, was not altogether at his ease. There are obvious signs that the hand that could already move with such courage and freedom, when the mere satisfying of himself was in question, was hampered by a return, partial at least, to his earlier timidity, when so much was at stake. He was so anxious to do his best that the spontaneity, conspicuous in most of his work, escaped in the process. The result is a little stiff in consequence, and the work somewhat dry and frigid; but the life and expression in the various heads is, nevertheless, so excellent, that it is impossible to regard it without delight and admiration.

Portraits again took up much of his time in 1633, among them the two companions to the portraits of the year before, and another pair, "Willem Burchgraeff," at Dresden [No. 1557], and "Margaretha van Bilderbeecq," his wife, in Frankfort [No. 182]. The painter's masterpiece, however, in matrimonial groups, is the "Shipbuilder and his Wife," at Buckingham Palace.


There are thirteen other signed portraits of that year, including one of "Jan Herman Krul," at Cassel [No. 213], two of "Saskia" – one at Dresden [No. 1556]; one, called however, "Lysbeth van Rijn," which belonged to the late Baroness Hirsch-Gereuth – and two of himself, one, the oval portrait in the Louvre [No. 412], and the other in the collection of M. Warneck at Paris. Out of these 5twelve signatures, only one is the monogram R.H.L., the other eleven being signed with the full name, and from only one of these, "A Head of a Girl," in the collection of Prince Jousoupoff, is the d missing.

Three subject-pictures also belong to that year, in all probability; "An Entombment," in the Hunterian Museum, Glasgow; a small picture described as "Petitioners to a Biblical Prince," belonging to M. Léon Bonnat of Paris; and "A Philosopher in Meditation" [No. 2541], in the Louvre. The last, indeed, though undated, may almost certainly be attributed to that year, since its companion, another "Philosopher in Meditation," also in the Louvre [No. 2540], is signed R. van Rijn, 1631. But the great event of the year must have been the patronage which came to him from Prince Frederick-Henry, resulting in the purchase of two pictures, both of which, in later years, after passing to the gallery at Düsseldorf, were transferred to Munich.

In both we see Rembrandt at his most characteristic – his determination to tell his story clearly, to concentrate his light upon the chief figure, the keynote of his theme, to get the true and expressive actions of his personages, not even yet free of some exaggeration, without troubling a jot as to the minor detail of correct costume. So, in the first, "The Elevation of the Cross" [No. 327], the cross, with the tense figure wrung with anguish, slants right athwart the picture, and stands out against the murky sky and dim surrounding crowds with startling incisiveness. So the four men occupied in raising it display an almost passionate energy; so a soldier wears a more or less classical helmet and breastplate over a sleeved doublet unknown to Rome; a man behind is dressed in the peasant's ordinary garb of Rembrandt's day; and another, wearing a doublet and soft flat cap, seems to be Rembrandt's self; while the centurion on horseback superintending the carrying out of the sentence is a frank Turk as to his headgear, a nondescript for the rest of him. The other, "The Descent from the Cross" [No. 326], while displaying many of the same qualities, merits and defects alike, is more deliberately composed, suffers indeed from that over-composition already noticed, being too obviously built up into that high pyramidal form, which we found in "The Presentation in the Temple." There is, nevertheless, a very delicate sentiment of pathos in it, and that Rembrandt himself was content with it, is shown not only by his correspondence with Huygens on the subject, but by the fact that he repeated it on a larger scale during the following year. Yet so curiously capricious was he in adding or withholding date and signature that neither has a date, and only "The Descent from the Cross" is inscribed with what appears to be C. Rlembrant f.

# CHAPTER VI

# TIME OF PROSPERITY (1634-1642)

At the one hundred and twenty-nine pictures produced during the succeeding nine years I can only glance hastily. There are eighteen works dated 1634, and, no less than seven of them are, or are called, "Portraits of Himself." One at the Louvre [No. 2553], and two at Berlin [Nos. 808 and 810], are unmistakably so, and one now in America, a companion to a "Portrait of Saskia," would seem to be; but the "Portrait of Rembrandt as an Officer," at the Hague [No. 149], which, however, bears no date, and one in a helmet, at Cassel [No. 215], bear only the most general resemblance to him. He furthermore painted a portrait of "Saskia disguised as Flora," called "The Jewish Bride," in the Hermitage at St Petersburg [No. 812], a very similar picture in the collection of M. Schloss, Paris, and a third at Cassel [No. 214]. There are eight dated portraits, and one probably belonging to that year. Among the portraits are the pair to the one of "Dr Tulp," and two other pairs, "Martin Daey" and "Machteld van Doorn," his wife, belonging to Baron Gustave de Rothschild, and "The Minister Alenson" and "His Wife," belonging to M. Schneider, Paris, a "Portrait of Himself in a Cuirass," in the Wallace collection, one of "A Young Girl," at Bridgewater House, and the "Old Lady," in the National Gallery [No. 775]. There are also four subjects. A replica of "The Descent from the Cross," formerly in the Cassel Gallery, but removed by Napoleon I. to Malmaison, whence it passed to the Hermitage [No. 800]. It is of interest historically as showing that high as Rembrandt's reputation stood at the time, he had leisure enough to paint this large picture, without any immediate purchaser in prospect, and it remained in fact on his hands until the enforced sale in 1656. A second, also in the Hermitage [No. 801], is "The Incredulity of St Thomas," and a third, in the Prado at Madrid [No. 1544], has been called both "Queen Artemisia receiving the Ashes of Mausolus" and "Cleopatra at her Toilet." There is also a doubtful "Tobias restoring his Father's Sight," in the collection of Duc d'Arenberg at Brussels, but it is a matter of doubt whether the last figure of the date is 4 or 6. Lastly, there is an undated "Prodigal Son," belonging to the executors of the late Sir F. Cook, which, in spite of the signature, must also be regarded as dubious.

There are only two "Portraits of Himself" dated 1635, and one of "Saskia," but there are two others attributed to about that time, and, in addition, two large and highly finished pictures, supposed to represent "Rembrandt and Saskia," both signed Rembrandt, and believed to have been painted in or near that year. The one at Dresden [No. 1559], contains, without doubt, portraits of the painter and his wife. The other, at Buckingham Palace, long known as "The Burgomaster Pancras and his Wife," is less certain.

Apart from these, there are nine dated portraits, and five subject-pictures, together with six portraits and one subject of about the date. Only two of the portraits bearing dates are in public galleries, one "A Rabbi," at Hampton Court [No. 381], and one "A Man," in the National Gallery [No. 350], while two others of about the date are the "Portrait of Himself," in the Pitti [No. 60], and "A Young Woman," at Cassel [No. 216]. In subjects the artist on two occasions went out of his way to court failure in attempting to represent classical subjects, with the spirit of which he was utterly out of sympathy. The homely truthfulness of his art, though it may occasionally result in details somewhat shocking to the reverent mind, was, nevertheless, well adapted to set forth the humanising side of Scripture incidents. His Christ is always more the Son of Man than the God Incarnate. His Virgin Mary has none of the delicate beauty conceived for her by Italian painters, but she is first of all, and beyond all, the type of motherhood. His apostles have none of the heroic dignity of Michelangelo's, yet they are without question devout, devoted fishers of men. But this lack of wish or power to idealise, this persistence in the search for the true and neglect of the beautiful, is entirely at variance with the classical tradition. There are no great fundamental ideas beneath the story of "Actæon, Diana, and Callisto," or "The Rape of Ganymede," for the artist to bring home to us, and the representation of the former as coarse, ungainly peasants, as in the picture belonging to Prince Salm-Salm of Anholt, or of the latter as a fat and extremely hideous baby boy blubbering in terror as he is howked upwards – no more dignified phrase will express it – by his shirt-tail in the claws of an eagle, as in the picture at Dresden [No. 1558], serve only to reveal the limitations of the artist's imagination without disguise or compensation.

Three other subject pictures, painted in or about that year, are also in public galleries: a little sketch of "The Flight into Egypt," at the Hague [No. 579]; "The Sacrifice of Abraham," in the Hermitage [No. 792]; and "Samson threatening his Father-in-law," at Berlin [No. 802].

Seven pictures only bear the date 1636, of which one formed a further addition to the collection of Prince Frederick-Henry, – "The Ascension," now at Munich [No. 328], quite the least satisfactory of the series. Rembrandt, indeed, was not in a happy vein this year in his treatment of subjects. Both the "Samson overpowered by the Philistines," in the collection of Count Schönborn at Vienna, and Lord Derby's "Belshazzar's Feast," if it be Rembrandt's, which, though unsigned, is attributed to that year, are seriously marred by a distinct melodramatic element in the conception, an extreme exaggeration of pose, gesture, and expression. On the other hand, we find the most pleasing study of the nude the painter ever made, in the "Danae," at the Hermitage [No. 802], which, though the first and third figures of the date have disappeared, leaving only two sixes, was most probably painted that year.

The four remaining pictures are portraits; two, forming a pair, a young man and his wife, belonging to Prince Liechtenstein of Vienna; one, a woman, to Mr Byers, Pittsburg, U.S.A.; and also a woman, to Lord Kinnaird. The "Ecce Homo," in the National Gallery [No. 1400], must have also been painted that year, if not before, for it is a sketch for the etching of that date. Other pictures probably dating from that year are a "Standard Bearer," belonging to Baron Gustave de Rothschild, from which the last figure of the date is missing; a "Portrait of an Old Lady," belonging to the Earl of Yarborough; "A Saint," formerly in the collection of Earl Dudley; "Saint Paul," at Vienna; and the "Portrait of an Oriental," in the Hermitage [No. 813].

1637 is inscribed on eight pictures, but in one case, that of a "Portrait of Himself," belonging to Captain Heywood-Lonsdale, there is some doubt about the correct reading of the last figure, and in that of "Susannah and the Elders," in the collection of Prince Jousoupoff, the genuineness of the signature is not above suspicion. No such question, however, applies to the rendering of the same subject at the Hague [No. 147], the "Portrait of Himself," in the Louvre [No. 2554], the "Portrait of Henry Swalm," at Antwerp [No. 705], that of another "Minister" at Bridgewater House, or to the "Portrait of a Man," in the Hermitage [No. 811], once absurdly called "Sobieski," and now, with scarcely less absurdity, said to be Rembrandt. The remaining work is "The Parable of the Master of the Vineyard," also in the Hermitage [No. 798]. Two portraits, one of himself, belonging to Lord Ashburton, and one of a "Young Woman" lacing her bodice, belonging to Dr Bredius, are also attributed to that year, as is "The Angel quitting Tobit," in the Louvre [No. 2536], in which once more Rembrandt's desire for actuality has, as far as the angel is concerned, led him to the border-line between the ungraceful and the ridiculous.

In the following year we find him for the first time attempting pure landscape. One, signed and dated, an entirely imaginary composition, is in the possession of Herr Georg Rath at Buda-Pesth; another, also signed and dated, in which he has to some extent compromised by introducing some small figures illustrating the "Parable of the Good Samaritan," is in the Czartoryski Museum at Cracow. "Christ and Mary Magdalene at the Tomb," in Buckingham Palace, though the figures are made of more importance, may also be included in the transition pictures between landscape and subject, for the garden, tomb, and distant city are at least as much insisted on as the figures. The important picture of the year, however, was a figure subject, "Samson propounding his Riddle to the Philistines," the great canvas in the Dresden Gallery [No. 1560], a magnificent piece of work, but, apart from its technical qualities, of no great interest: the only other pictures dated 1638 being a "Portrait of an Old Man," in the Louvre [No. 2544], and a "Bust of a Man in Armour," at Brunswick [No. 237].

Two more pictures were completed for the Stathouder in 1639, a "Resurrection" [No. 329], signed and dated, and an "Entombment" [No. 330], unsigned, now with the others at Munich. The only other subject treated that year, if the date and signature are genuine, which M. Michel doubts, was "The Good Samaritan" dressing the wounds of the injured man, in the collection of M. Jules Porgès, for "The Slaughter-house," belonging to Herr Georg Rath, is a study rather than a picture; and the "Man with the Bittern" at Dresden [No. 1561] as much a portrait as a study. Other portraits are the so-called "Lady of Utrecht," lent by the family Van Weede van Dykveld to the Amsterdam Museum; that of "Alotte Adriaans," belonging to the executors of the late Sir F. Cook, a life-sized full-length figure of "A Man," at Cassel [No. 217], at one time erroneously called "Burgomaster Six," and a so-called "Portrait of Rembrandt's Mother," at Vienna [No. 1141].

There are six pictures dated 1640 – four subjects and two portraits – one of himself in the National Gallery [No. 672], and the famous one of "Paul Doomer," better known as "The Gilder," now in the possession of Mr Havemeyer of New York. The subjects include the Duke of Westminster's beautiful "Salutation" and the "Expulsion of Hagar and Ishmael," in the Victoria and Albert Museum, in both of which, however, the concentration of light on a small portion is so intense as to suggest the lime-light of a theatre; the charming version of "The Holy Family" in the Louvre [No. 2542], known as "The House of the Carpenter," where the contrasting light and shade, though equally marked, are reasonably brought about; and the mysterious allegory, in the Boymans Museum at Rotterdam [No. 238], known as "The Concord of the Country," containing a rather confused mass of detail and incident, all obviously meaning something, but what no one can quite decide.

Other pictures supposed to have been painted about the same time are a "Good Samaritan"; a "Saving of Moses," in which the figures play a part quite subordinate to the landscape; three pure landscapes, "An Effect of Storm," at Brunswick [No. 236], one in the Wallace collection; a study of "Dead Peacocks," belonging to Mr W. C. Cartwright; and several portraits, the most noteworthy of which is the one of "Elizabeth Bas" in the Ryksmuseum at Amsterdam [No. 249].

Six pictures again bear the date 1641, and all are portraits except the great "Offering of Manoah and his Wife," at Dresden [No. 1563], wherein we are distressed once more by the artist's unfortunate conception of an angelic being. Two of the portraits form a pair now widely sundered, the admirable "Lady with the Fan" being at Buckingham Palace, while her husband has strayed away to Brussels [No. 397]. The portrait of "The Minister Anslo" – a marvel of life-like expression and superb painting – is a sad example of art treasures which have been allowed to leave England of late years, having passed from Lady Ashburnham to Berlin. The "Portrait of Anna Vymer," on the other hand, the mother of Burgomaster Six, is one of a very few, if it be not the only one, which is still in the possession of the descendants of the subject. The remaining picture is a portrait of a Young Woman, called "Saskia," at Dresden [No. 1562].

The dated pictures of 1642 are few. There is one subject in the Hermitage [No. 1777] long known as "The Reconciliation of Jacob and Esau," but now recorded in the catalogue as "The Reconciliation of David and Absalom"; while the "Christ taken from the Cross," in the National Gallery [No. 43], may belong to the same year, since it is a sketch probably made for the etching which was certainly executed then. There are also four portraits: one of "A Rabbi," belonging to M. Jules Porgès of Paris; Lord Iveagh's "Portrait of a Woman"; Mrs Alfred Morrison's "Portrait of Dr Bonus"; and "An Old Man," at Buda-Pesth [No. 235].

This limited production was probably due to the fact that a large share of his time must have been taken up by his largest and most famous work, "The Sortie of the Company of Francis Banning Cocq," for many years known as "The Night-watch," because time and careless usage had so blackened it that the original illumination was nearly obscured, and the figures appeared to be dimly visible by artificial light. The careful restoration by M. Hopman has, of late years, altered all this, and that the sortie is taking place by daylight, the condensed, highly localised daylight of Rembrandt, to be sure, has been established beyond cavil.

One would have supposed that such devoted art-patrons as the Dutch people of that time, would have hailed with delight the creation of such a masterpiece by one of themselves, and would have showered praises and commissions upon its creator. The very contrary seems to have been the fact; nor is the reason far to seek.

Holland at that time abounded in Guilds and Companies, civil and military, Boards of Management of this or that Hospital or charitable Institution, and a perfect craze for being painted in groups animated one and all. The galleries are full of these

"Doelen" and "Regent" pictures by great and little masters, and dreary objects many of them are. Each member subscribed his share, and each expected to get his money's-worth; so the painter was expected to distribute his light and his positions with an impartial hand, and a comically stiff and formal collection of effigies was often the result.

To all such considerations Rembrandt was gloriously indifferent. He was painting a picture of an event in real life, and he meant it to be a picture and alive, not a mere row of wax figures in a booth; and when he had finished, the subscribers cried aloud in wrath and consternation.

And indeed it is difficult not to sympathise with the poor amateur soldiers who had paid to be painted, not to be immortalised. Even if they could have known, they would have cared very little for the fact that their picture was to rank in after years among the most famous in the world, since their worthy citizen-faces were not to be discerned in it, and no one would care to read the names which, failing to move the domineering painter, they caused to be inscribed upon an escutcheon in the background so that they might get some return for their florins. They had their revenge, however, after a kind, for they left it to blacken with dirt and smoke; and when their descendants removed it from the Doelen to the Hotel de Ville they cut it down ruthlessly on either hand to make it fit a smaller space, as a copy by Lundens in the National Gallery [No. 289] makes evident.

# CHAPTER VII

# YEARS OF DECLINE (1643-1658)

There is still no lack of portraits in 1643. There are two pairs, "The Gentleman with the Hawk," and "The Lady with the Fan," at Grosvenor House, which, however, Dr Bode and M. Michel decline to admit among Rembrandt's works, and "The Dutch Admiral" and "His Wife," now in America. It is doubtful whether the "Old Woman weighing Money," at Dresden [No. 1564], ought to be included among the portraits; but there can be no question about the "Young Man in a Cap and Breastplate," in the same gallery [No. 1565], the "Old Woman," in the Hermitage [No. 807], called "Rembrandt's Mother," or the "Man," in the collection of Mr Armour. The other "Old Man," belonging to Mr Schloss of Paris, is probably only a study; and the "Portrait of a Man," incorrectly called Six, in the collection of Morris K. Jessup of New York, is but conjecturally a work of this year. There are three portraits of himself: one at Weimar, one belonging to Prince Henri of the Pays Bas, one, signed but undated, at Carlsruhe [No. 238]; and there is a portrait, called Saskia, at Berlin [No. 812]. The only signed subject of the year is the "Bathsheba at her Toilet," in the Steengracht collection at the Hague; but "The Holy Family," at Downton, was painted about that time.

The next year has very small results to show, and might, taken by itself, support the belief in the sudden unpopularity of Rembrandt were there not five other years for which we can now find only five pictures, and several with fewer. All the five of 1644 are signed. Three are portraits: Captain Holford's "Man with a Sword," Earl Cowper's "Young Man," and the fancifully named "Constable of Bourbon," in the collection of Herr Thieme at Leipzig. There is one subject-picture, "The Woman taken in Adultery," painted for Jan Six, and now in the National Gallery [No. 45]. Another of the same subject, in the possession of Consul Weber at Hamburg, bears, according to M. Michel, a forged signature, and is regarded by him as very doubtful.

There are four subject-pictures dated 1645. First and foremost is "The Holy Family," in the Hermitage [No. 796]. Fine also is "The Tribute Money," belonging to Mr Beaumont, though much more summarily handled. The "Daniel's Vision," at Berlin [No. 806], is more careful in treatment, but the companion picture, "Tobias' Wife with the Goat" [No. 805], is little more than a sketch. At Berlin, also, are two of the five dated portraits of that year, one of "A Rabbi," in the Museum [No. 828A], and one of "J. C. Sylvius," in the collection of Herr von Carstangen. The Hermitage has one portrait [No. 820], called at one time "Manasseh ben Israel." A "Portrait of a Young Girl," in the Dulwich Gallery [No. 206], and "An Orphan Girl of Amsterdam," now in the United States, are probably works painted for the purpose of study, rather than portraits; and the same remark applies to the "Portrait of Himself," at Buckingham Palace, which, though the last figure of the date is wanting, was, in all likelihood, a work of that year.

The "Portrait of a Lady," in the collection of Captain Holford; the little sketch of "An Old Man Seated," belonging to the executors of the late Sir F. Cook, and "An Old Man," at Dresden [No. 1571], are undated portraits of about this time; while the "Man reading by a Window," in the Carlsberg Glyptotek at Copenhagen, if it be really a Rembrandt, which is doubtful, is an undated subject. There are, furthermore, two landscapes, both undated, one at Oldenburg [No. 169], and one in the collection of Mme. Lacroix at Paris.

Another landscape, "A Winter Scene," at Cassel [No. 219], is dated 1646, as is a "Portrait of a Young Man," belonging to Mr Humphry Ward. There are also four subject-pictures bearing the same date, two of "The Adoration of the Shepherds," one in the National Gallery [No. 47], painted originally for Six, and one at Munich [No. 331], differing entirely in arrangement; one of "Christ bound to the Column," in the collection of Herr von Carstangen at Berlin; and the "Holy Family," called "The Woodchopper," at Cassel [No. 218].

1647 is inscribed on only five pictures. Two are the portraits called "Nicholas Berchem," and "His Wife," at Grosvenor House, and a small one of "An Old Man," at Leeuwarden, in the collection of Baron van Harinxma. A fourth of "Dr Bonus," in the Six collection, is not dated, but as it exactly resembles the etching of that year, it is, with much reason, attributed to it. There is only one subject, "Susannah and the Elders," in the Berlin Gallery [No. 828E]. Two undated studies also belong to about that time, a small head and shoulders of "Susannah," belonging to M. Léon Bonnat of Paris, and the "Woman bathing," at the Louvre [No. 2550]. A large picture of "Joseph's Coat," in the collection of the Earl of Derby, is one of the most ungraceful and undignified spectacles that even Rembrandt's stern realism ever produced. Enchanting, on the other hand, in its truth and delicacy is the "The Shepherds reposing at Night," in the National Gallery of Ireland, with its contrasted effects of firelight and moonlit night.

No known portrait bears the date 1648, though one of "A Young Painter with Papers and Crayon," signed Rembrandt 164 –, is believed to belong to about that year. There are, however, four dated subject-pictures: two at the Louvre – "Christ at Emmaus" [No. 2539], and "The Good Samaritan" [No. 2537], – one, "Hannah teaching the Infant Samuel to read," at Bridgewater House, and one, a different version of "Christ at Emmaus," at

Copenhagen [No. 292]. A small picture of "Christ on the Cross," in the collection of Herr Carl Hollitscher at Berlin, was also probably painted about this time.

he succeeding year, 1649, is one of the two that has no dated picture, and were it not for the "Portrait of Marshal Turenne," at Panshanger, which must have been painted that year – if indeed it be his, which has recently been doubted – we should have to regard it as utterly barren; for M. Jules Porgès' "Old Woman" is only supposititiously of that date. We may be sure, however, that some of the large number of unsigned pictures attributed to about that time were undoubtedly painted in the course of it. Of these there are several in public galleries: "The Slaughter-house," at Glasgow [No. 707], from the date on which the two last figures are missing; the portrait of "His Brother," in the Emperor Frederick Museum at Berlin; the "Bust of an Old Man," at Strasburg; the "Portrait of Himself," at Leipzig; "The Ruin," at Cassel [No. 220]; the picture, called "The Metamorphosis of Narcissus," at Amsterdam [No. 1251]; and five pictures in the Hermitage: "Abraham entertaining the Angels" [No. 791], "The Sons of Jacob bringing him Joseph's Coat" [No. 793], "The Disgrace of Haman" [No. 795], "Pallas" [No. 809], and "Hannah teaching Samuel to read" [No. 822], none of which is dated, though the second, third, and fifth are signed. There are also in private hands, two portraits in those of M. Jules Porgès, a portrait in M. Bonnat's, and others. Dated pictures of the year 1650 are rare. There is a "Portrait of Himself," in the Fitzwilliam Museum at Cambridge, and one, "His Brother," at the Hague [No. 560]; and three subject-pictures, "Tobit and his Wife," the Duke of Abercorn's "Deposition," and "The Young Woman in Bed," in the National Gallery, Edinburgh.

The same number of pictures is dated 1651. Four are portraits: one of himself, belonging to Herr Mendelssohn of Berlin; the "Old Man," in the possession of the Duke of Devonshire; "The Man with a Baton," in the Louvre [No. 2551], and "The Girl with a Broom," in the Hermitage [No. 286]. The subject-picture "Christ and Mary Magdalene in the Garden," called "Noli me tangere," is at Brunswick [No. 235].

The next two years are very deficient in dated pictures. Two only, "The Old Man," seated in a chair, belonging to the Duke of Devonshire, and the "Portrait of Bruyningh," at Cassel [No. 221], are dated 1652; but the picture of "Hendrickje Stoffels," in the Louvre [No. 2547], and a "Head of Christ," belonging to M. Rodolphe Kann of Paris, are of about that year. 1653 has only one, "The Portrait of a Man," wrongly entitled Van der Hooft, belonging to the Earl of Brownlow, for "The Entombment," at Dresden [No. 1566], is but a copy of the picture at Munich [No. 330], touched up by Rembrandt. Here again we may safely accord to the seemingly empty year some of the undated pictures of the period, which include six portraits, one of which, "An Old Man," is in the Hermitage [No. 818]. "An Old Woman," in the same collection [No. 804], may also belong to the year, for it is very similar to the two pictures, dated the following year [Nos. 805 and 806]. The only other undated pictures which call for special mention are two landscapes: the "Mill," in the collection of the Marquis of Lansdowne, and the one at Glasgow [No. 705], which is known as "Tobias and the Angel" from the figures in the foreground.

The dated pictures of 1654 are nine portraits and two subjects, "Bathsheba," at the Louvre [No. 2549], being one, and "The Woman bathing," at the National Gallery [No. 54], the other. Of the portraits, one of himself, doubted, however, by Dr Bode, is at Munich, [No. 333], "An Old Man with a Beard," at Dresden [No. 1567], "An Old Woman," at Brussels [No. 397A], "An Old Jew," "An Old Man," and "An Old Woman," besides the two old women being in the Hermitage [Nos. 810, 823, and 825], while "The Young Servant" is at Stockholm [No. 584]. Most, if not all of these, however, were studies painted because his still restless energy would not allow him to be idle. The same may be said of the portraits dated 1655, only two of which we can even suppose to have been commissions – the companion pictures of "An Old Man," and "An Old Woman," at Stockholm [Nos. 581 and 582];

the two others bearing dates being studies of his son "Titus," one in the collection of M. Rodolphe Kann, the other in that of the Earl of Crawford. The dated picture at Glasgow [No. 706], like the undated "Man in Armour," at Cassel, is rather a study of armour than a picture. The portrait at the Louvre [No. 2546], a copy of one at Cassel [No. 225], and the rest of the undated heads, mostly of small size, painted about that time, are simply sketches or studies, the only subjects being "The Slaughter-house," in the Louvre [No. 2548], and two pictures of "Joseph accused by Potiphar's Wife," differing only in details, one at Berlin [No. 828E], and one in the Hermitage [No. 794], for "The Flight into Egypt," at Buda-Pesth, though belonging to the period, is undated.

1656, the year of his actual bankruptcy, was an unusually prolific one, including "The Anatomy Lesson of Dr Johannes Deyman," now in the Ryksmuseum at Amsterdam, of which, unfortunately, the fire of 1723 has left only a fragment, [No. 1250]; the "Portrait of Arnold Tholinx," belonging to Madame André-Jacquemart of Paris; the "Portrait of an Architect," at Cassel [No. 224], the signature and date of which, however, M. Michel declares to be forged; and the companion pictures of "A Young Man," and "A Young Woman," at Copenhagen [Nos. 273 and 274], the second of which is alone dated. There are also two undated "Portraits of Himself," painted about that time – one belonging to Lord Iveagh, the other to Lady de Rothschild; and an "Old Man," at Dresden [No. 1568]. In addition to these portraits there are two large subject-pictures – "The Parable of the Labourers in the Vineyard," at Frankfort [No. 181], and "Jacob blessing Joseph's Sons," at Cassel [No. 227], besides "The Preaching of St John the Baptist," at Berlin [No. 828K]. There are, moreover, two pictures belonging to about that date – "The Denial of St Peter," in the Hermitage [No. 799], and "Pilate washing his Hands," in the collection of M. Sedelmeyer at Paris.

One, or perhaps both of these, may belong to the following year, 1657, which is otherwise lacking in important works, though it includes the "Portrait of Catrina Hoogh," known as "The Lady with the Parrot," belonging to Lord Penrhyn; "The Adoration of the Magi," at Buckingham Palace; a "Portrait of an Old Woman," belonging to M. Rodolphe Kann; and one, at Dresden [No. 1569], of "A Man sketching in a Book." It may also include the "Rabbi," in the National Gallery [No. 190], a "Portrait of a Boy," at Belvoir Castle, and "An Angel," a mere fragment of a larger picture, belonging to Mr Sellar.

1658 would seem to have been still more disastrous. Of three signed pictures, one is a "Portrait of Himself," in the collection of the Earl of Ilchester; one, "An Old Woman cutting her Nails," belonging to M. Rodolphe Kann, is undoubtedly a model; and only the "Young Man," in the Louvre [No. 2545], may be a portrait. Of the unsigned works of that time, two more are "Portraits of Himself," one belonging to Lord Ashburton, the other at Vienna [No. 1142], and one, also at Vienna [No. 1144], is probably a "Portrait of Titus," while two "Old Men," one of which is in the Pitti Palace [No. 12], are presumably models. The portrait, called "An Admiral," belonging to Mr Schaus of New York, and that of "Six," in the Six collection were, however, doubtless commissions. The subjects include one of Rembrandt's infrequent incursions into classical story in "Baucis and Philemon receiving Jupiter and Mercury," now belonging to Mr Yerkes of New York, a "Christ," in the possession of Count Orloff-Davidoff at St Petersburg, and Lord Wimborne's seated figure of "St Paul."

Few facts are more admirable in Rembrandt's checkered career than the noble struggle he maintained against misfortune and neglect. That he suffered there can be no doubt – the careworn face and whitening hair of the later portraits reveal it all too clearly, – but he stiffened his back and worked on undismayed.

Of 1659 there are six pictures fully dated, and two believed to have been, though in each the last figure of the date is missing. Both are "Portraits of Himself," one at Bridgewater House, and one at Cassel [No. 222], while a dated one, belonging to the Duke of Buccleuch, is a magnificent representation of the grave, strong face that had met and supported so much care. Three others are also portraits – "An Old Man," in the National Gallery [No. 243], the "Merchant," belonging to the Earl of Feversham, and "A Man in a Red Cloak," signed Rembran, in the collection of M. Maurice Kann at Paris. There are also two subject-pictures, both at Berlin, "Moses breaking the Tables of the Law" [No. 811], and "Jacob wrestling with the Angel" [No. 828].

To 1660 a large number of pictures is attributed, eighteen being portraits, and one, "Head of Christ," belonging to M. Maurice Kann, coming under the head of subject-pictures. Of these only four portraits are dated, and in two cases there is some doubt as to the last figure. Two of the dated portraits are of himself; one with the full date is in the Louvre [No. 2555], and one with a doubtful date belongs to Sir A. D. Neeld. Both are of extreme interest in their bearing on the personal history of Rembrandt. The portrait of the year before, belonging to the Duke of Buccleuch, shows us a man bearing some traces indeed of a struggle with adversity, but of a not altogether unsuccessful one. The character has been developed rather than shaken in the strife; the man is still strong in body, firm in mind; the hair, as far as it can be made out against the dark background, is still untouched by the hand of time; yet it is beyond question Rembrandt himself. In the two pictures now under consideration we find a change truly startling. The hair is thin and white, the face is wrinkled, the eyes weary. But it is in the character conveyed that the chief transformation is perceived; he has sunk suddenly into old age and weakness, the strength, the resolution of the man have gone out of him – he seems, stout as he was, to have broken at last. And yet in the next year he painted the finest work he ever did. There is nothing in his story to account for it. A severe illness seems the only possible explanation, followed by a remarkable, though brief, recuperation; but it is, perhaps, the greatest of the many great puzzles offered to us in the course of his history. Of the other two portraits, one, though fully signed and dated, is of a doubtful authenticity; while the date on "The Portrait of an Old Woman," belonging to Colonel Lindsay, is uncertain. The pictures painted about that year are numerous, and include a pair of portraits, husband and wife, belonging to Prince Jousoupoff; "The Capuchin," in the National Gallery [No. 166]; and two other figures in monks' robes, one belonging to Lord Wemyss, the other to Count Stroganoff; Captain Holford's portrait of a young man supposed to be "Titus"; "The Standard-Bearer," formerly at Warwick Castle but now transferred to America, and others.

There are ten pictures bearing the date 1661, one signed, but with the last figure of the date missing, and three with neither date nor signature. Of these, however, one, "The Conspiracy of Claudius Civilis," we know to have been painted that year. A second painted about the time is "The Circumcision," belonging to Earl Spencer. The third is the "Venus and Cupid," at the Louvre [No. 2543], if it should not rather be counted among the portraits, since Dr Bode believes it to represent Hendrickje Stoffels and her daughter Cornelia. The same doubt as to classification applies to the "St Matthew," also in the Louvre [No. 2538], and to "A Pilgrim at Prayer," belonging to Consul Weber at Hamburg. Two figures of "Christ," one at Aschaffenbourg, the other belonging to Count Raczynski at Posen, complete the list of subjects. There is only one "Portrait of Himself," belonging to Lord Kinnaird, the others being one of a man with a knife in his hand, nicknamed, "Rembrandt's Cook," at Downton; the "Portrait of an old Woman," in the Museum of Épinal; another "Old Woman," in the possession of Lord Wantage; "A Man," in the Hermitage [No. 821]; and the misnamed "Jansenius," belonging to Lord Ashburton. All other works of that year are, however, eclipsed by the artist's masterpiece, which, if it alone remained in existence, would compel us to place Rembrandt in the very highest rank of painters – "The Syndics of the Drapers," at Amsterdam [No. 1247].

After that eventful year, the record is a thin one. The very next, indeed, is the other of which no known picture survives. There are a pair of portraits, the "Man" in the collection of M. Maurice Kann, the "Woman" in that of M. Rodolphe Kann, which may have been painted that year; and the same may be said of a portrait called "Hendrickje Stoffels," at Berlin [No. 823B].

The next year is little better. A picture of "Homer reciting his Poems" alone bears part of a signature, and f., with the date 1663. It belongs to Dr Bredius, and is lent by him to the Museum at the Hague [No. 584]. 1664, again, is found on but one canvas, "The Death of Lucretia," belonging to M. Léon Gauchez of Paris, but "The Unmerciful Servant," in the Wallace collection, and the "Portrait of Himself," in the National Gallery [No. 221], belong to about that time. One, a "Portrait of an Old Man," in the Metropolitan Museum, New York [No. 274], is dated 1665. A portrait, signed Rembrandt f., in the collection of Mr Charles Morrison; one of himself, in that of Herr von Carstangen at Berlin; "The Jewish Bride," at Amsterdam [No. 1252], from the date on which the last figure is missing; and "David playing before Saul" were also painted about that year.

1666, however, appears on three portraits – "A Youth," belonging to Lord Leconfield; "A Woman," in the National Gallery [No. 237]; and "Jeremias de Decker," a poet who was one of Rembrandt's rare clients in his later years, at the Hermitage [No. 827]. The "Portrait of an Old Man," at Dresden [No. 1570], and two of himself – one at Vienna [No. 1143], signed but undated, and one in the Uffizi [No. 452] – were in all probability painted either that year, the one before, or the succeeding one, 1667, to which we can otherwise accord only one, a "Portrait of an Old Man," belonging to the Earl of Northbrook.

And now the tale is nearly told; 1668 occurs but once, on "The Flagellation," in the Grand-Ducal Museum at Darmstadt, absolutely the last known work of his; though three others – "Esther, Haman, and Ahasuerus," belonging to the King of Roumania; a large "Family Group," at Brunswick [No. 232]; and

"The Prodigal Son," in the Hermitage [No. 797], are believed to date from that year, or possibly even the next and last.

There is still a considerable number of pictures to which no very approximate date can be assigned, but as the attempt to fully consider all the work that Rembrandt did would far exceed all reasonable limits of space, I must reluctantly leave the reader who would seek further to such assistance as the catalogue of pictures at the end of this volume may afford him.

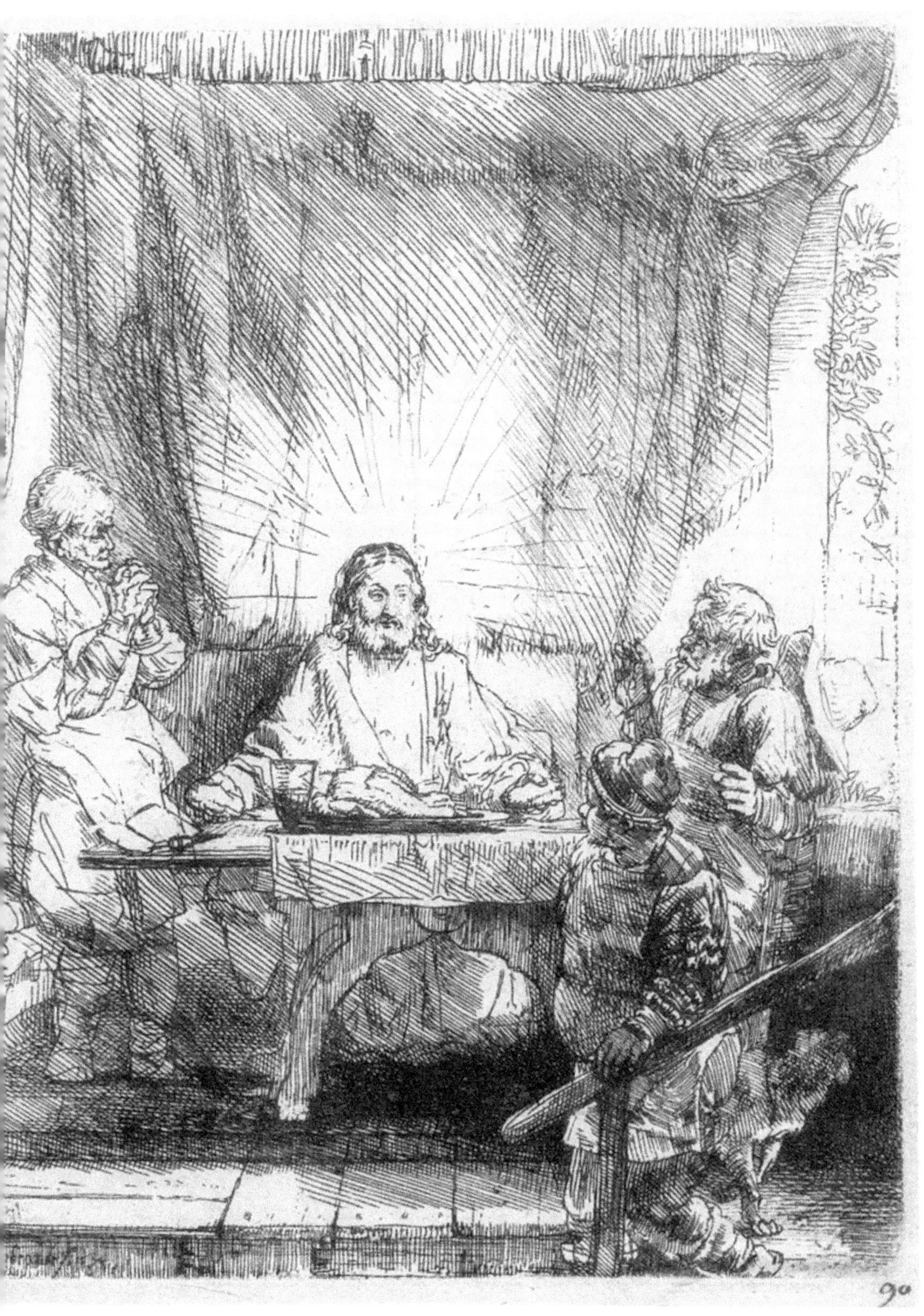

Rembrandt, Christ At Emmaus, 1654

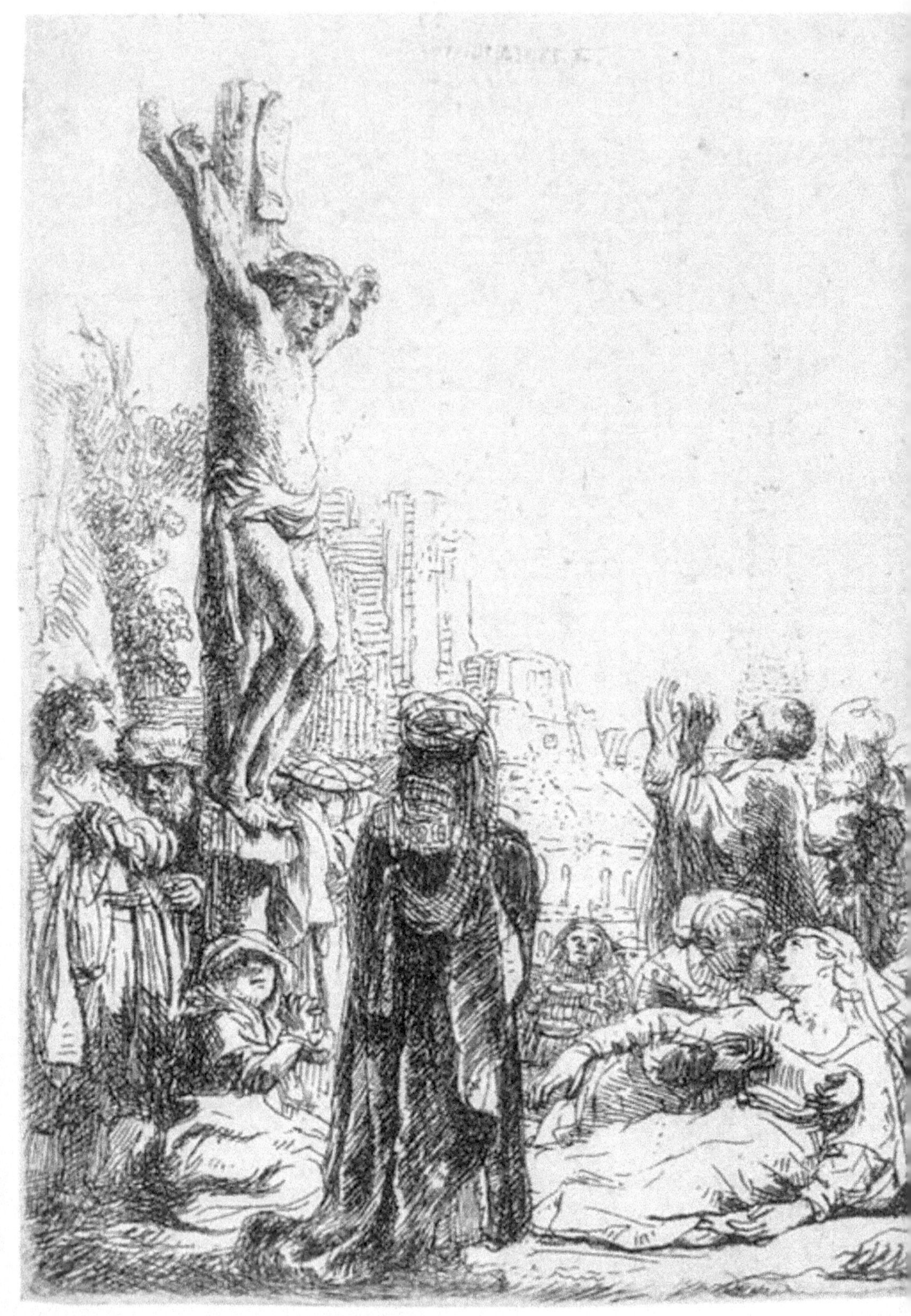

Rembrandt, The Crucifixion, 1637, Vienna

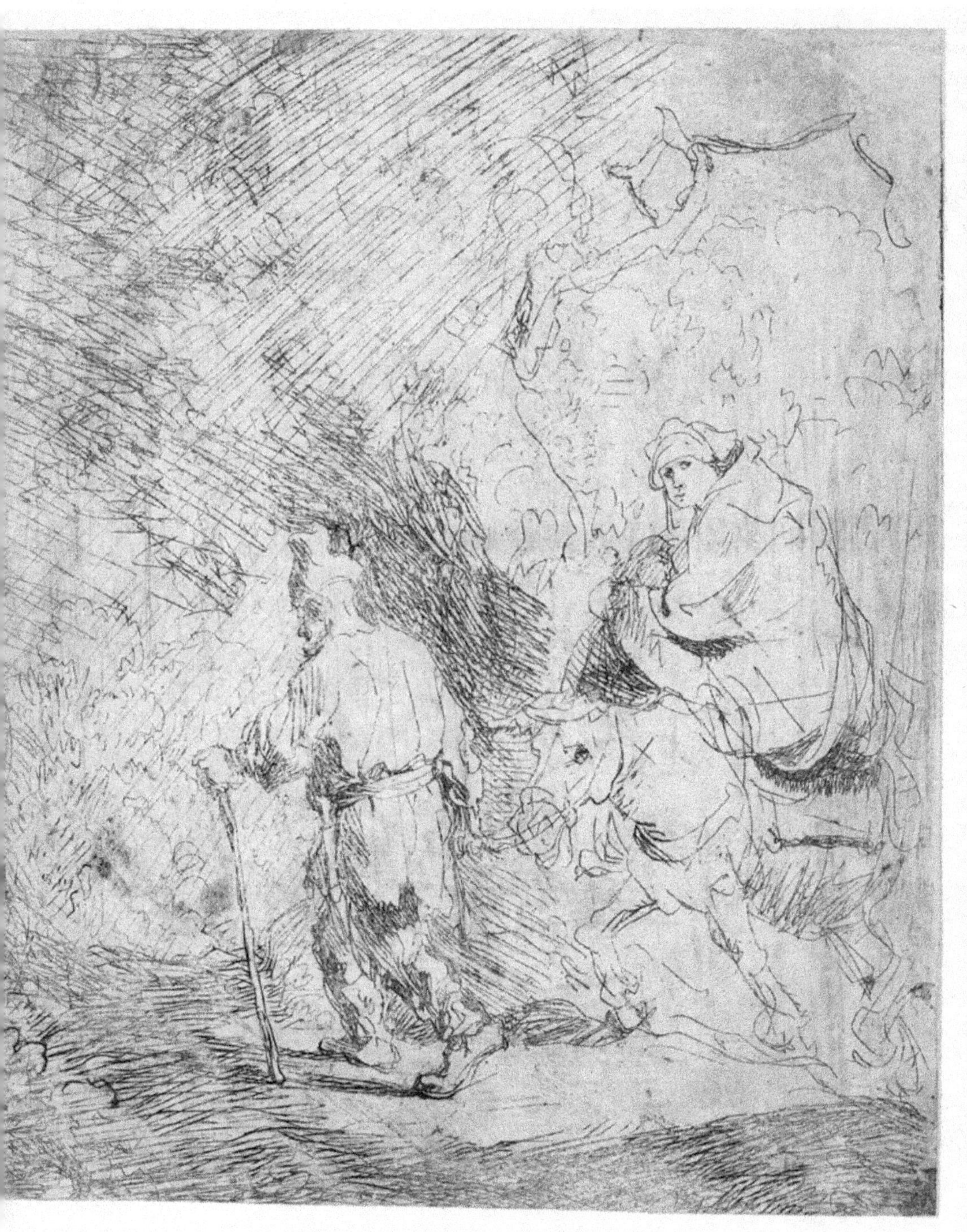

Rembrandt, The Flight Into Egypt, 1627, Rijksmuseum, Amsterdam

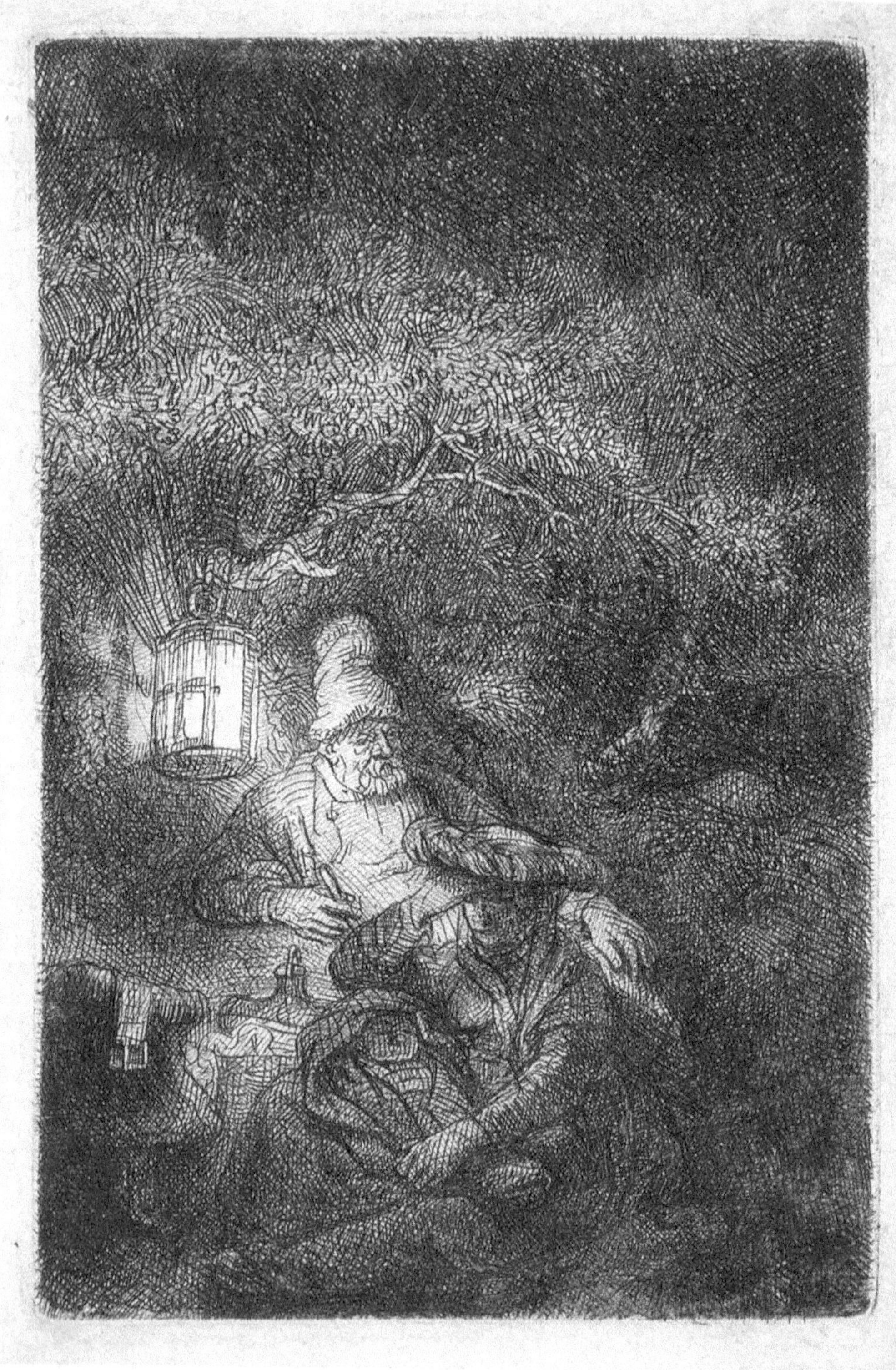

Rembrandt, The Rest on the Flight Into Egypt, Rijksmuseum, Amsterdam

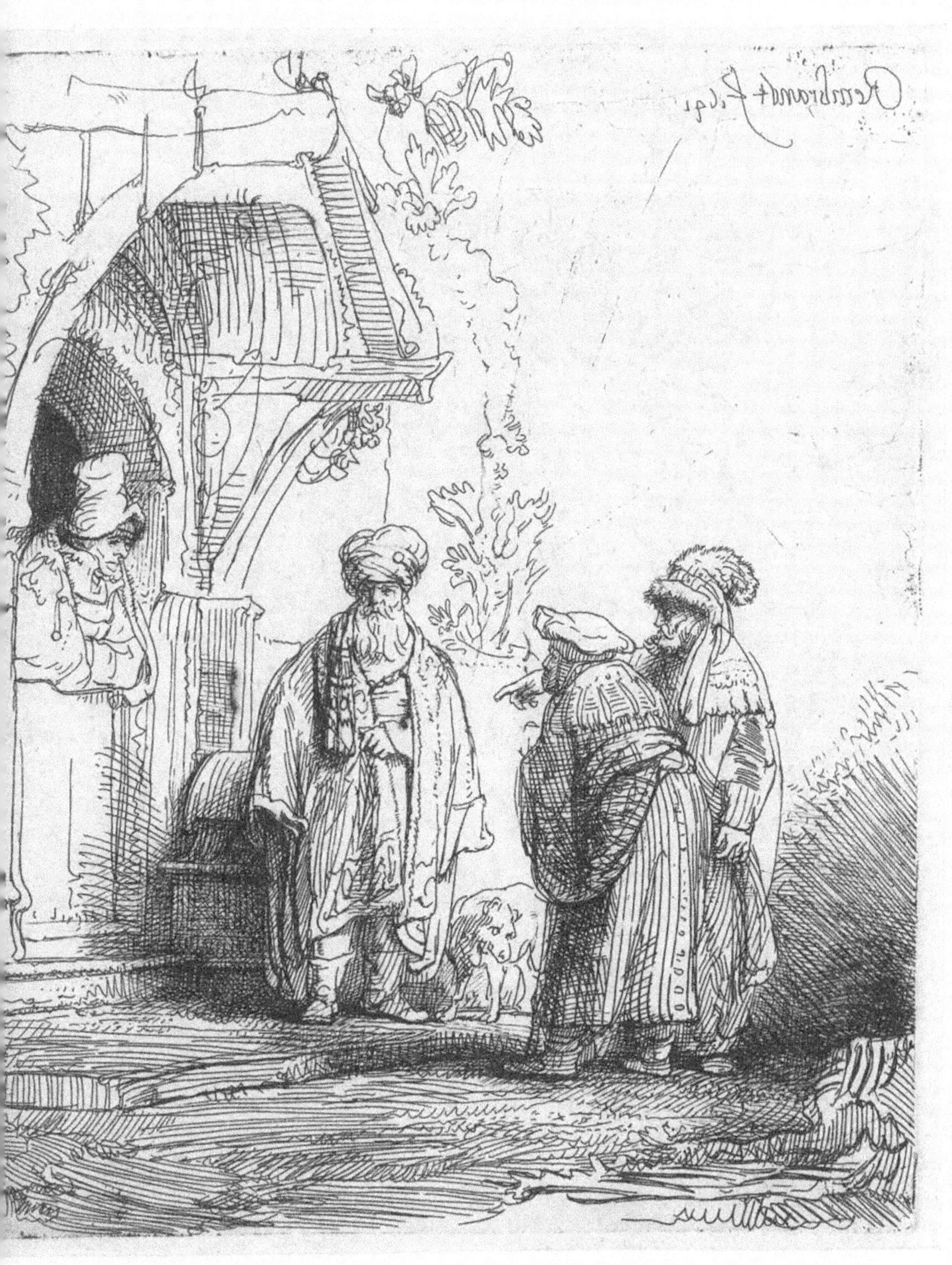

Rembrandt, Jacob and Laban, 1641, Rijksmuseum, Amsterdam

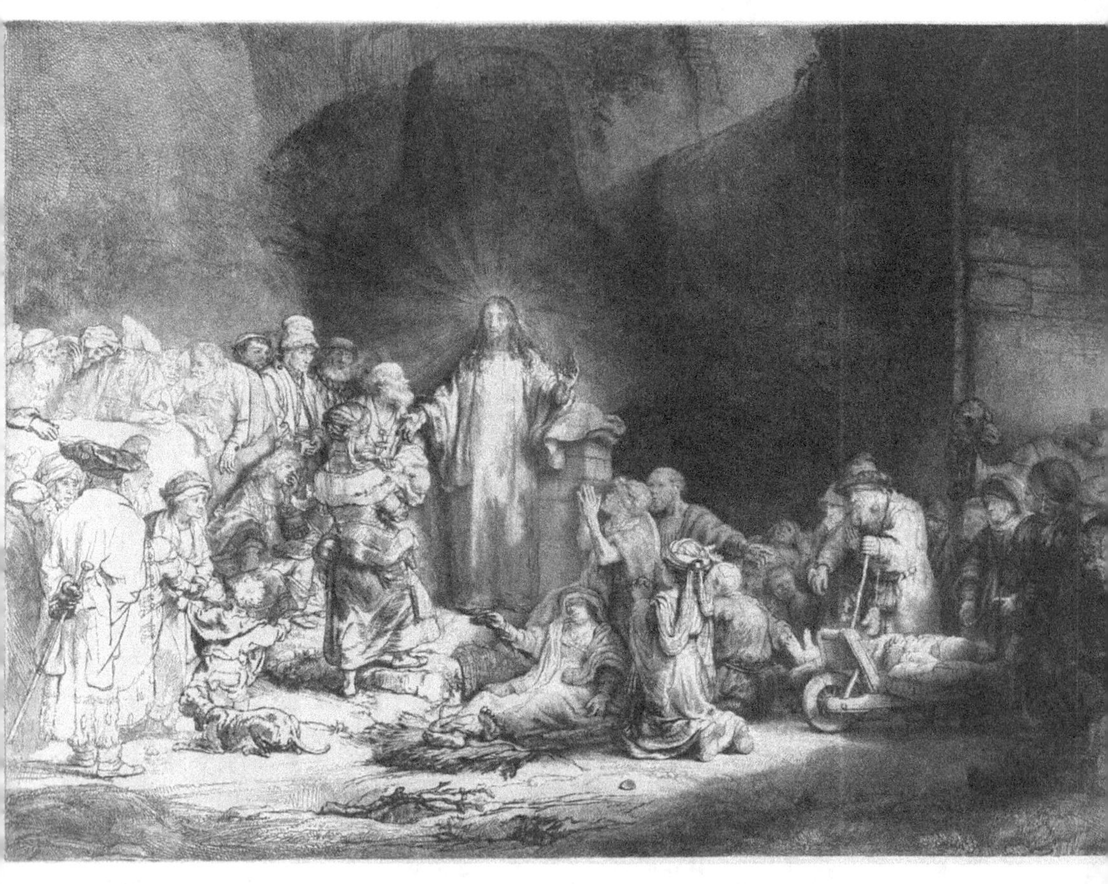

Rembrandt, The Little Children, 1646-50, Rijksmuseum, Amsterdam

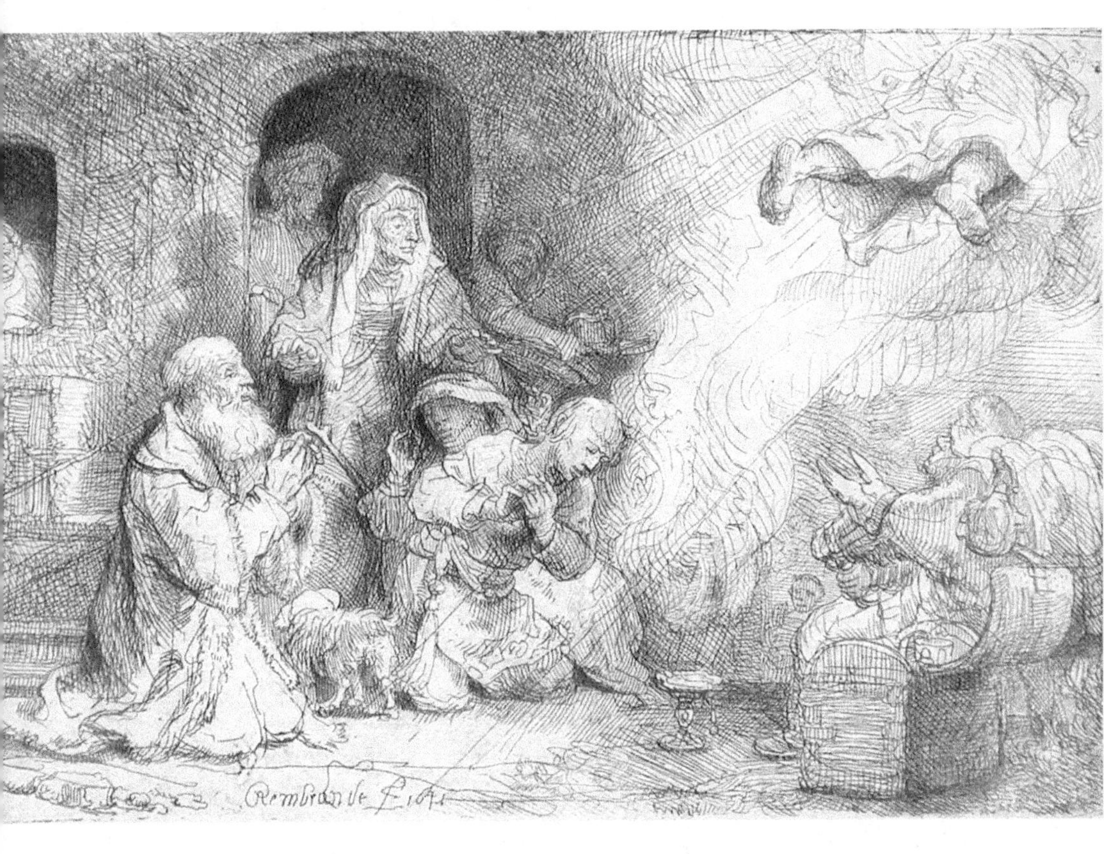

Rembrandt, The Angel Departing From the Family of Tobit, Los Angeles

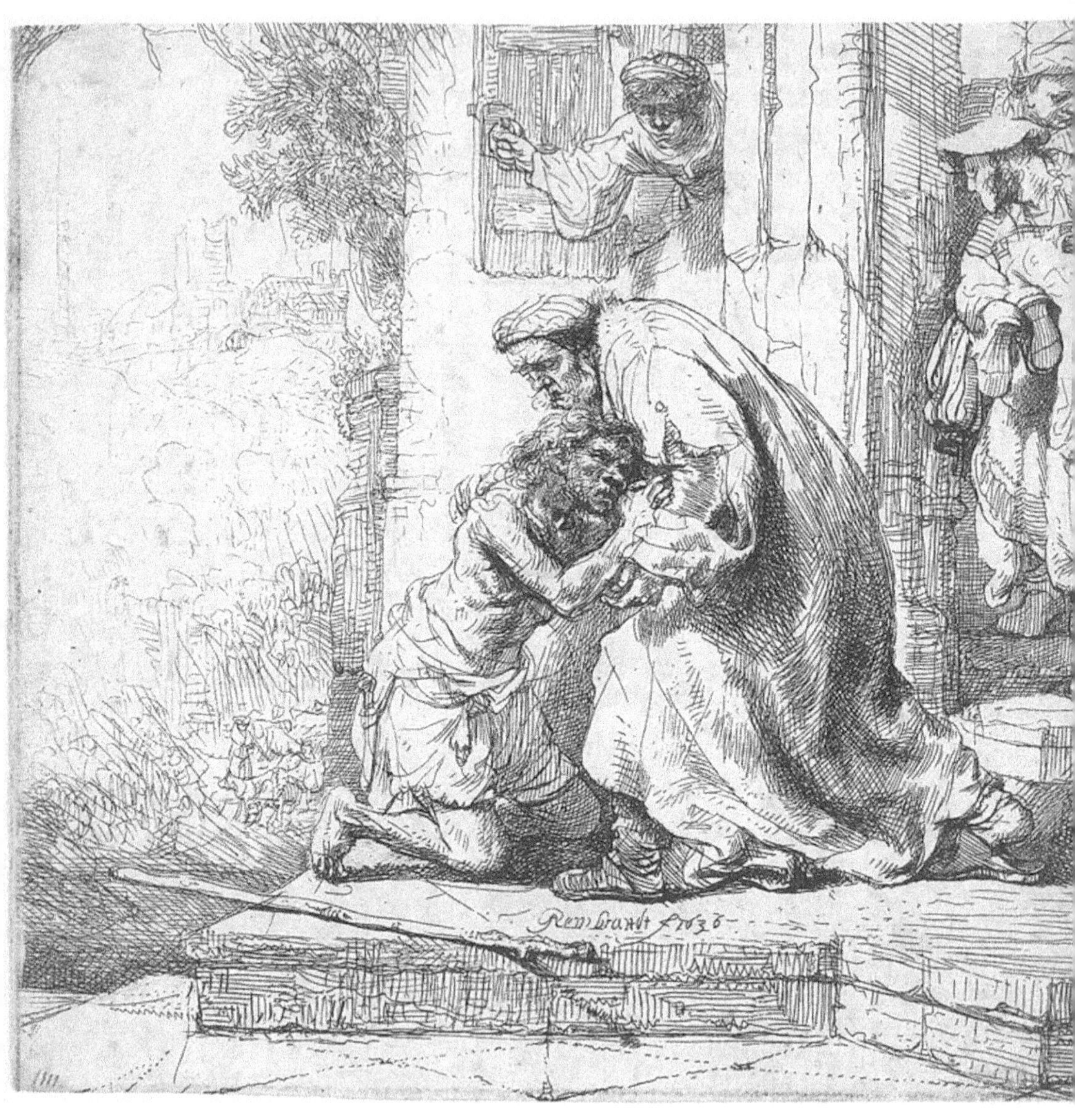

Rembrandt, The Return of the Prodigal Son, 1636, Rijksmuseum, Amsterdam

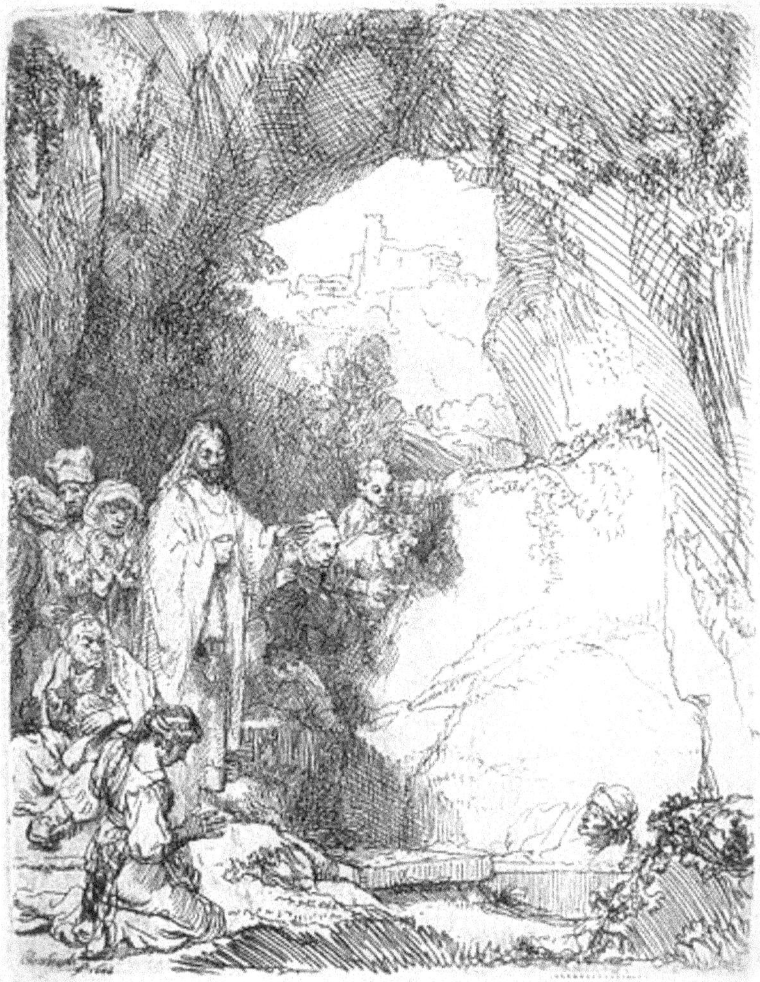

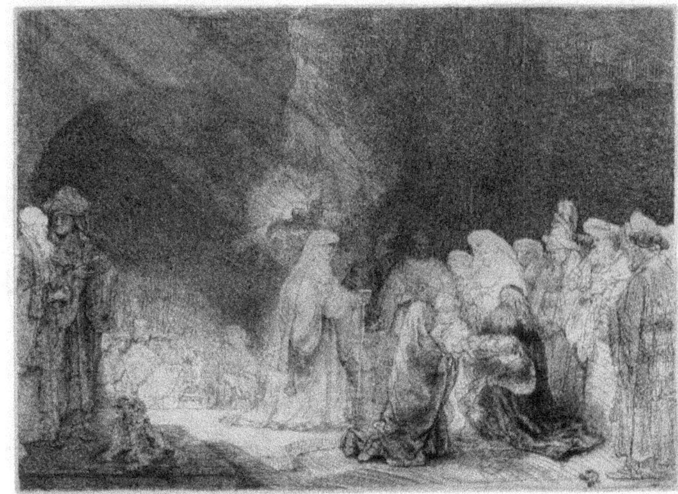

Rembrandt,
The Raising of Lazarus, 1642,
Rijksmuseum,
Amsterdam (above).
The Presentation In the
Temple, 1639,
British Museum (Right).

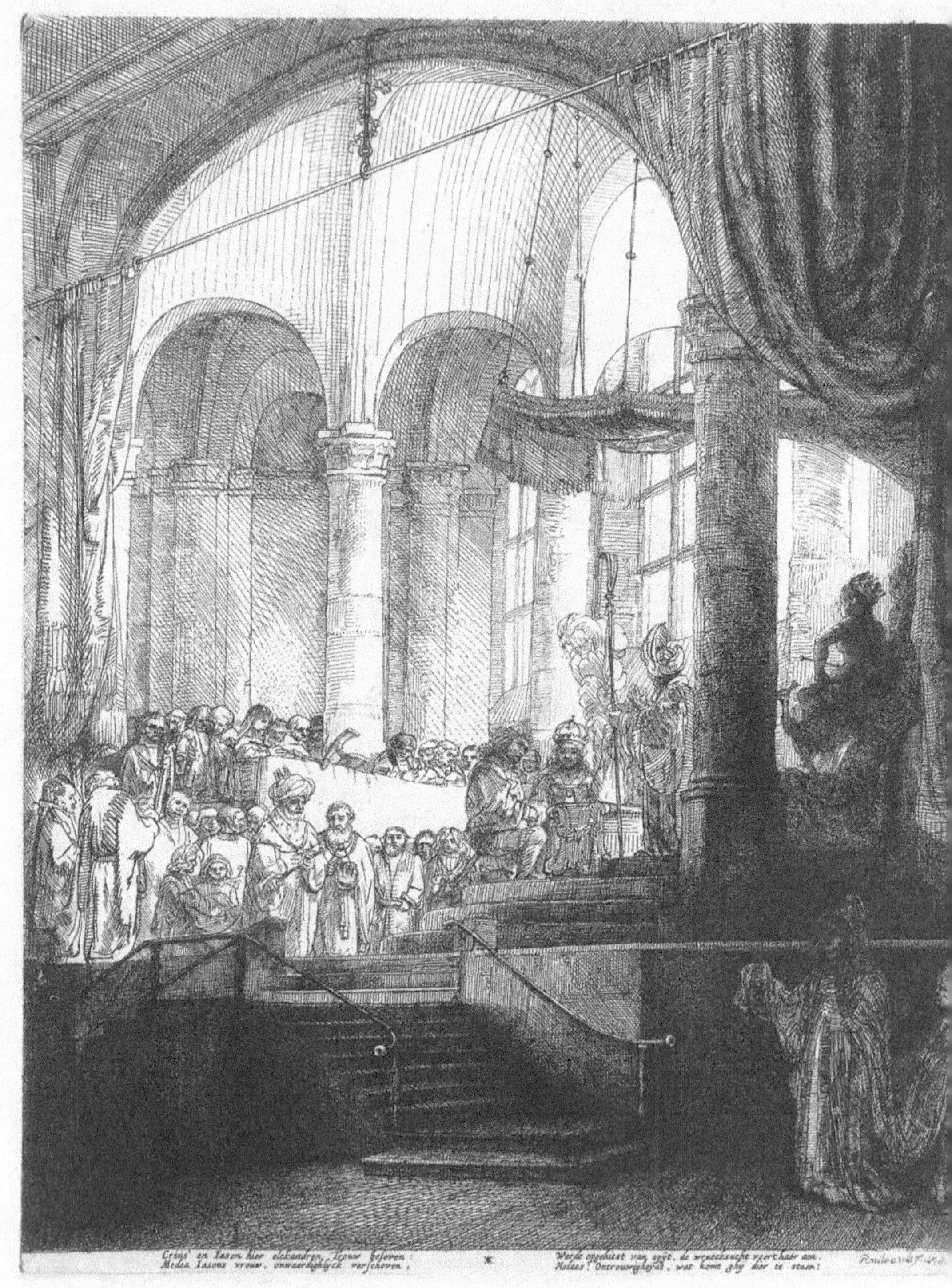

Rembrandt, Medea, 1648, Rijksmuseum, Amsterdam

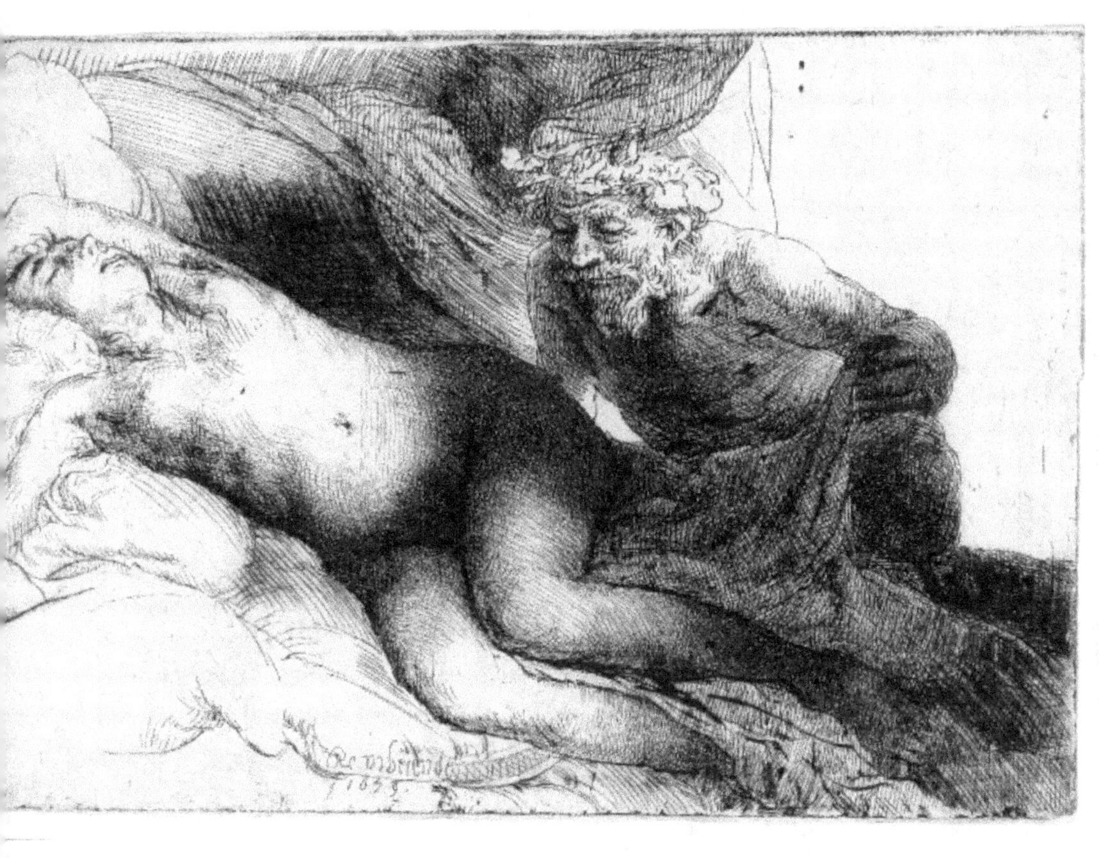

Rembrandt, Jupiter and Antiope, 1659, British Museum

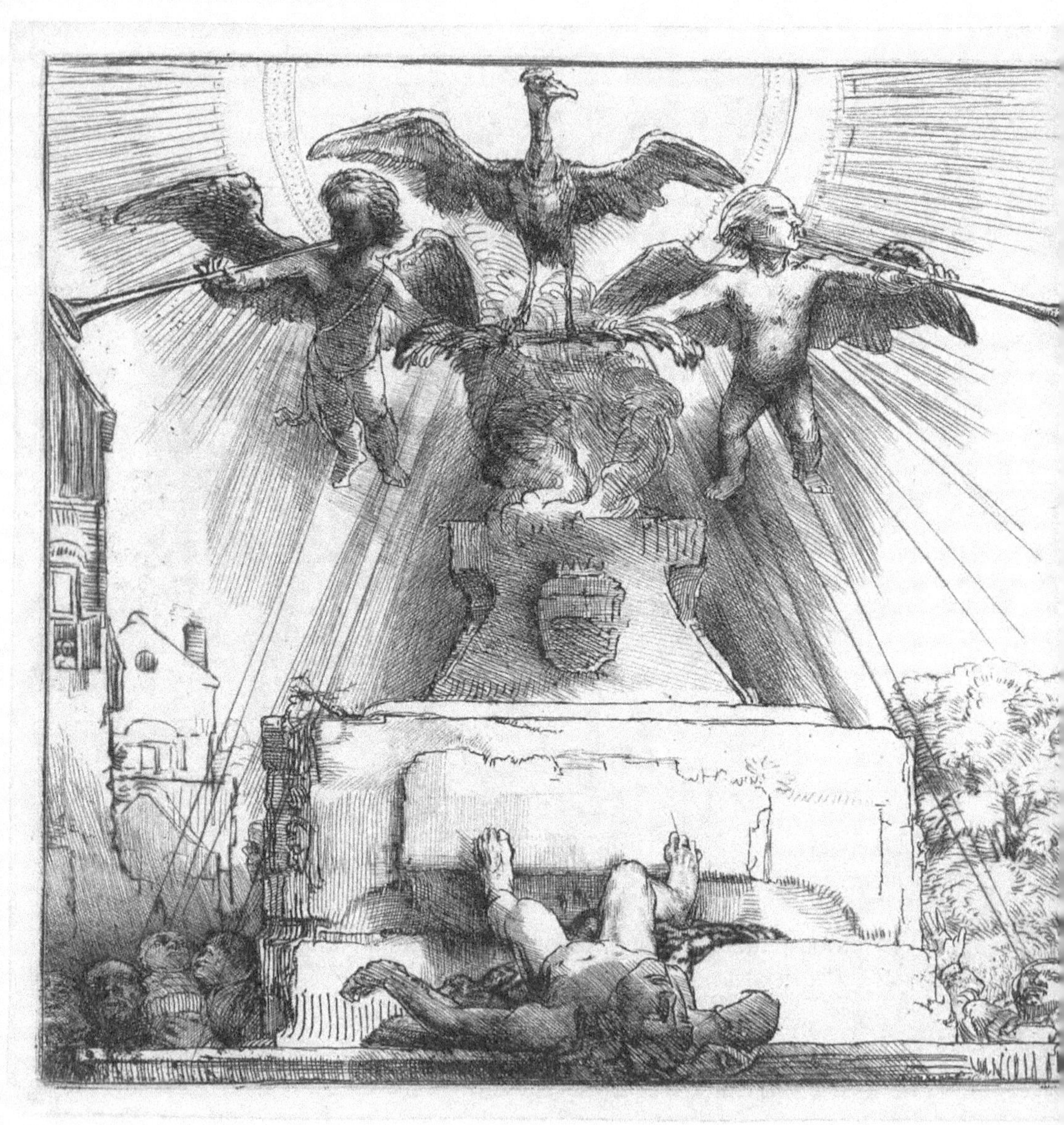

Rembrandt, The Phoenix, or the Statue Overthrown, 1658

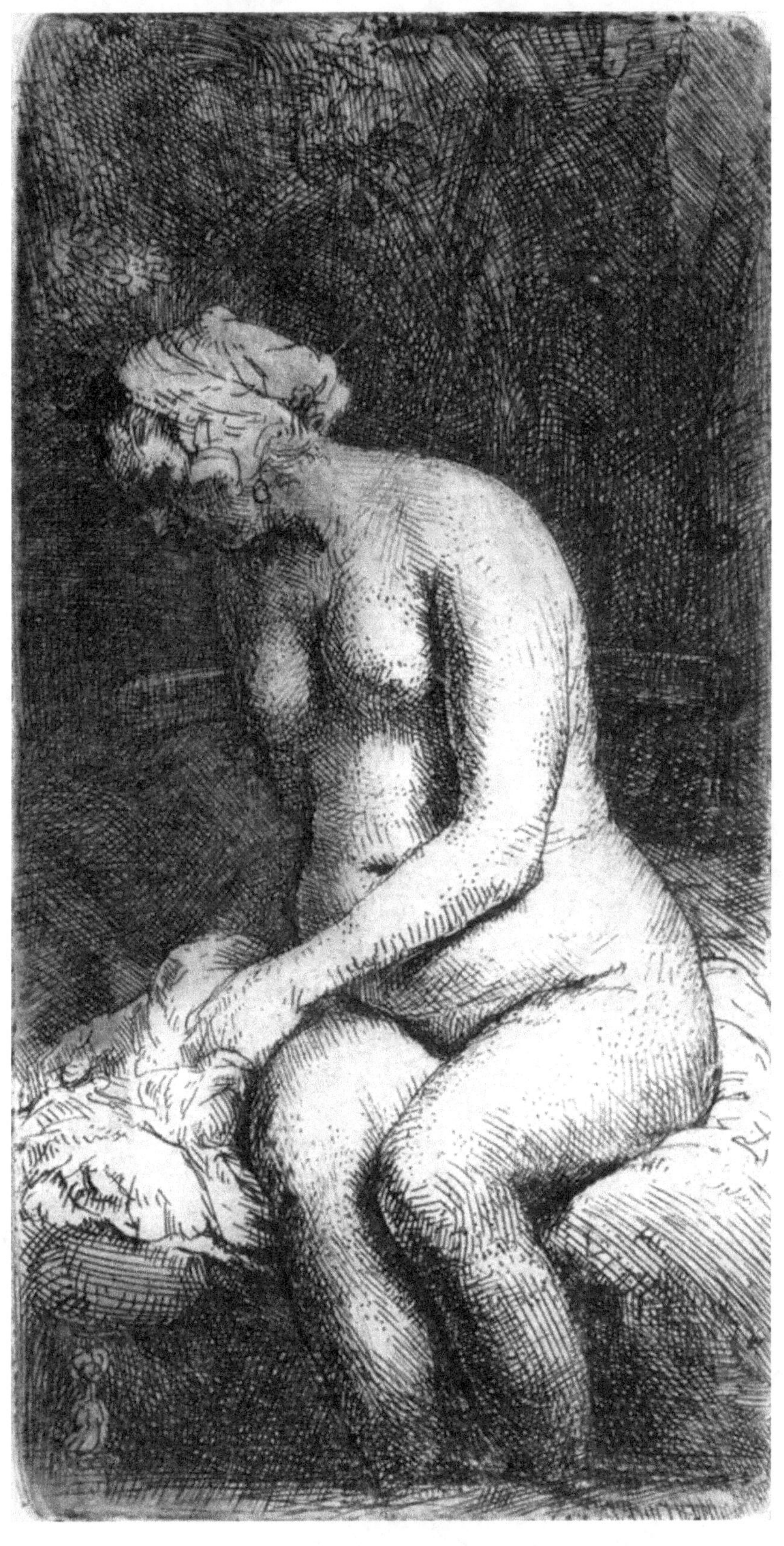

Rembrandt, Seated Nude, 1658

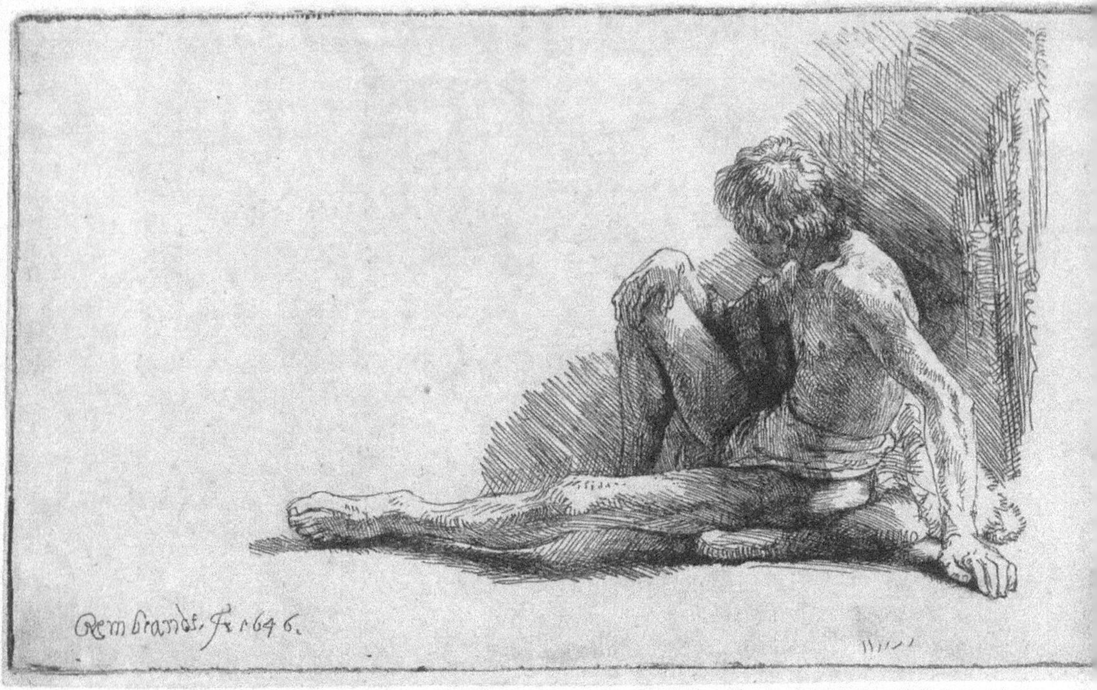

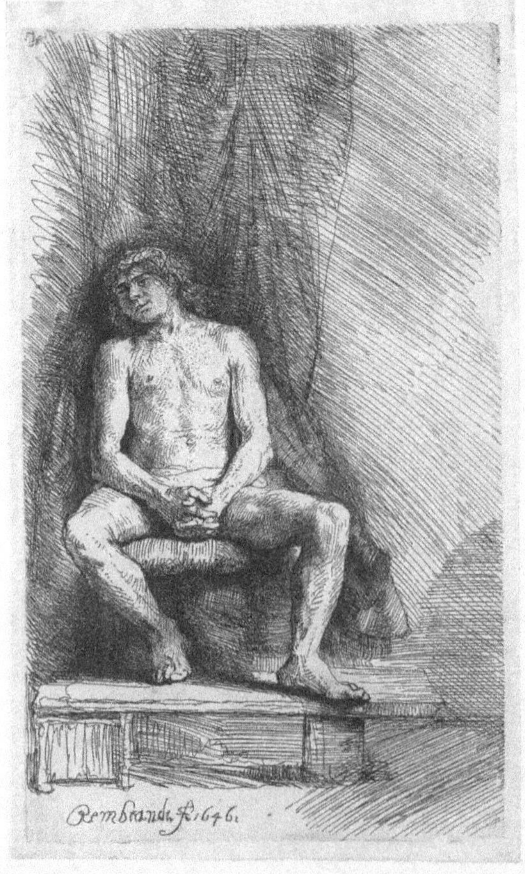

Rembrandt, Nude Man Seated,
1646 (above).
Nude Man Seated Before a Curtain,
Rijksmuseum, Amsterdam (left).

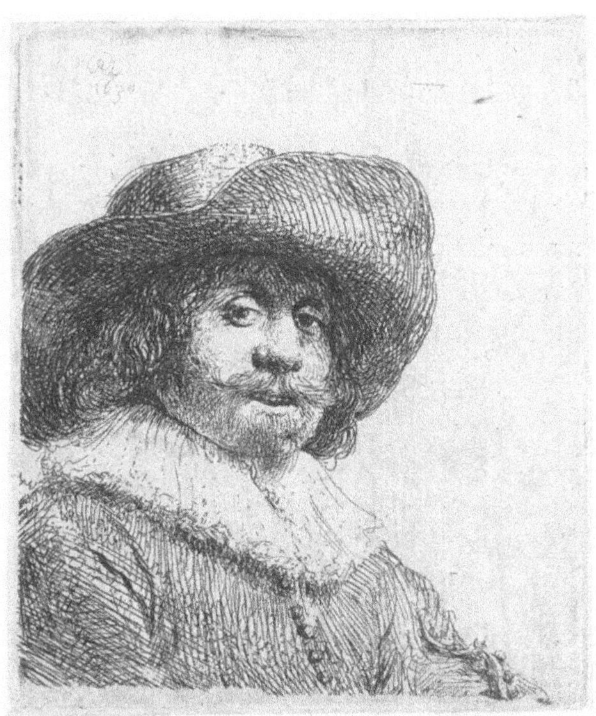

Rembrandt, Man In a Broad-rimmed Hat, 1638 (above).
Man At a Desk, 1641 (below). Both Rijksmuseum, Amsterdam.

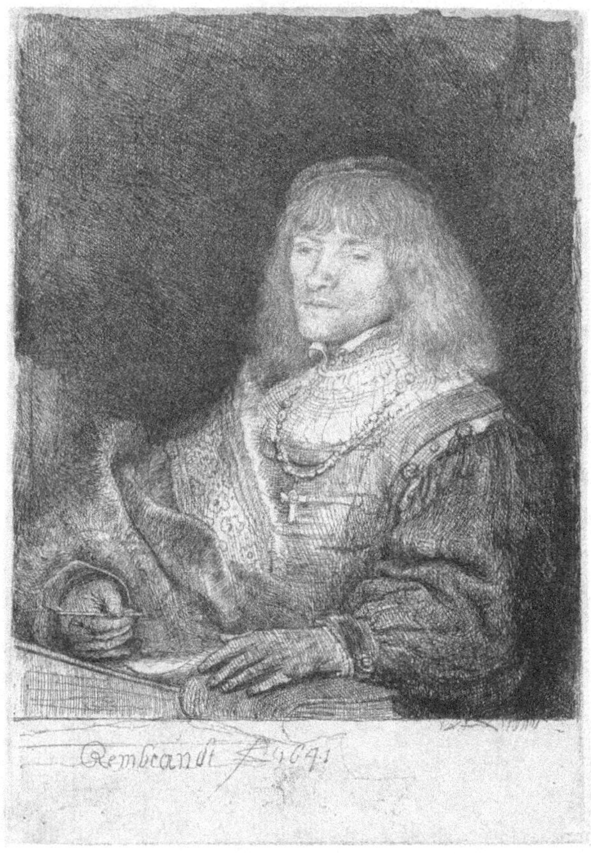

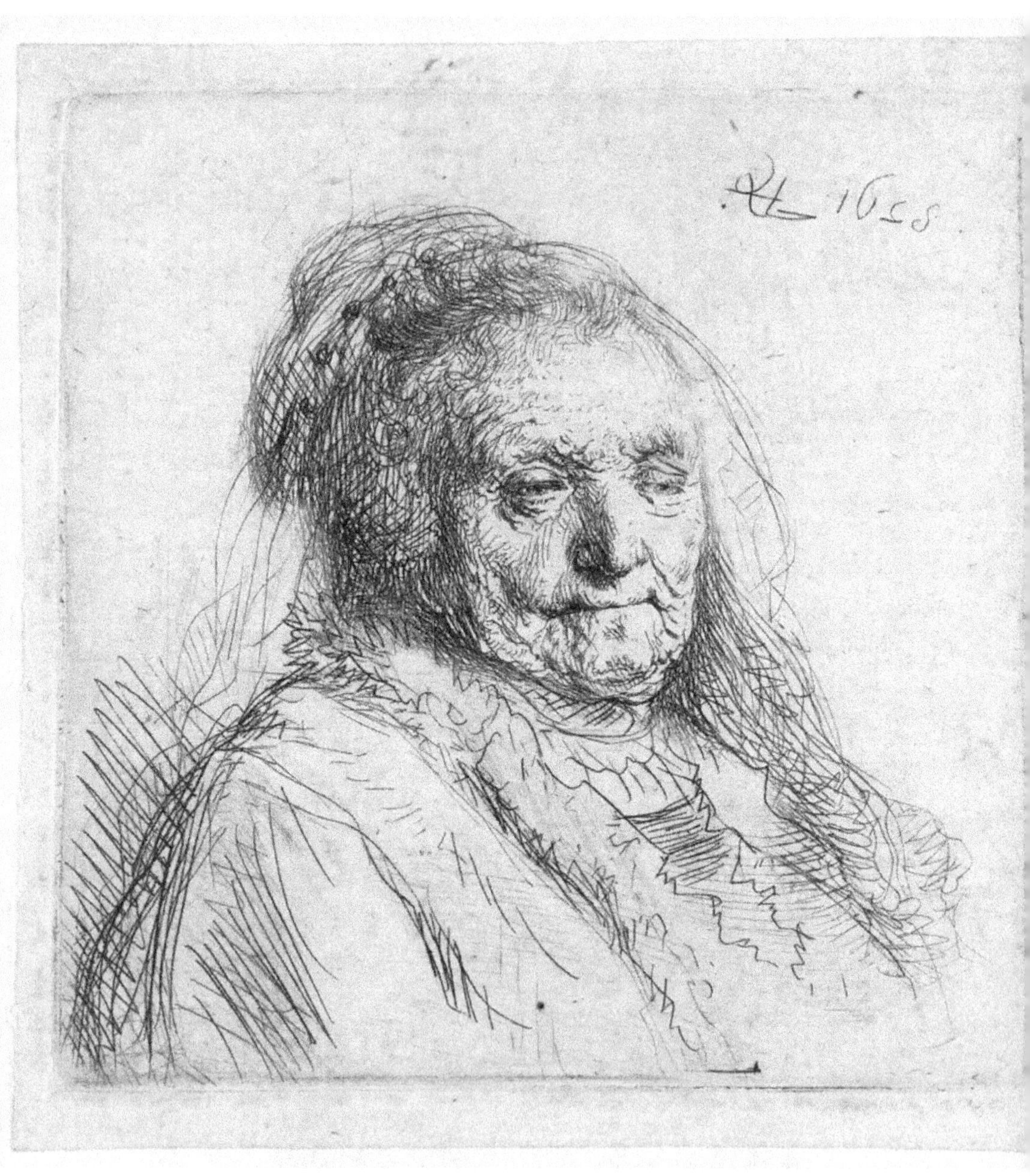

Rembrandt, Mother, 1628, Rijksmuseum, Amsterdam

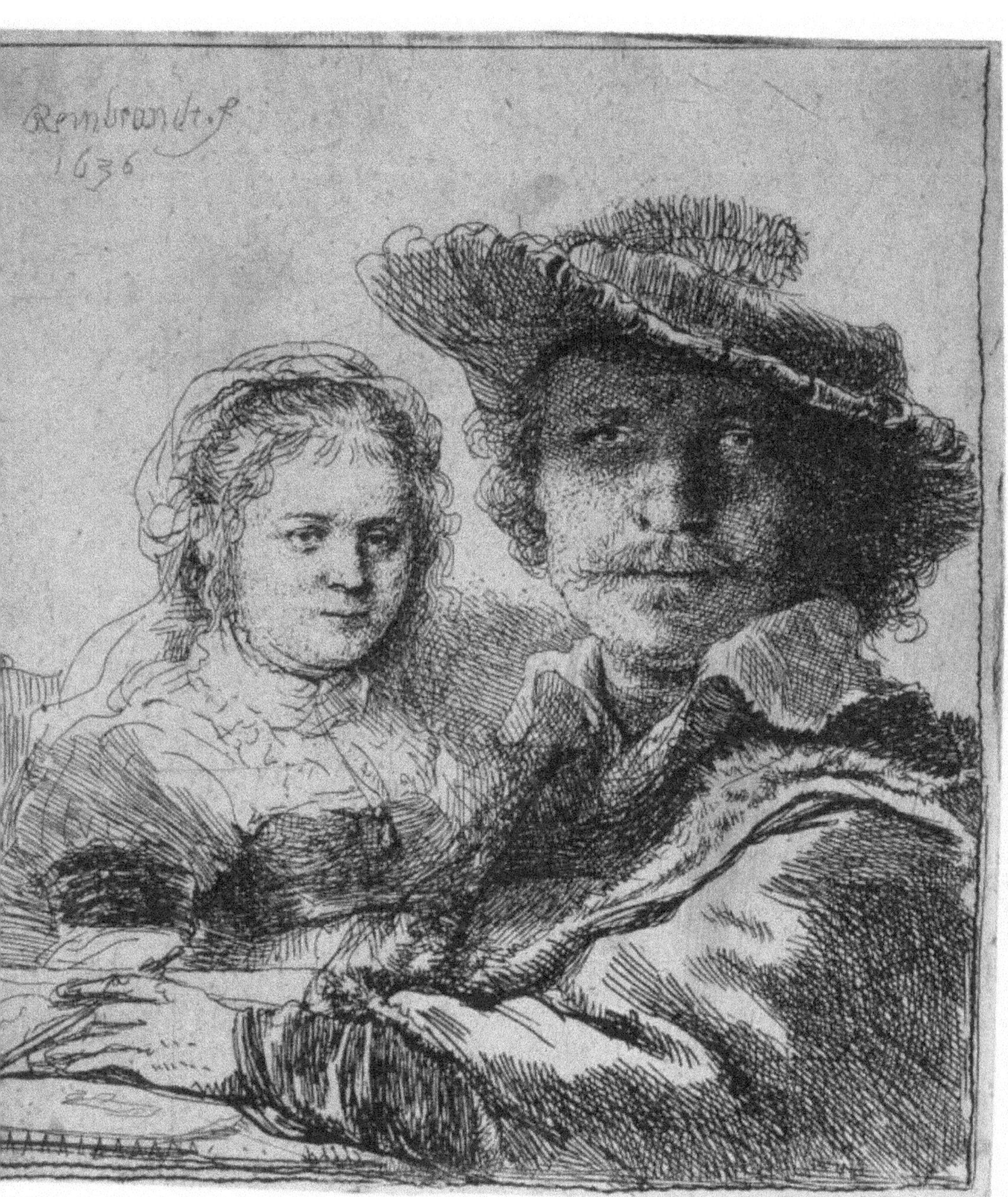



Rembrandt, Self-Portrait With Saskia, 1636, Hermitage Museum

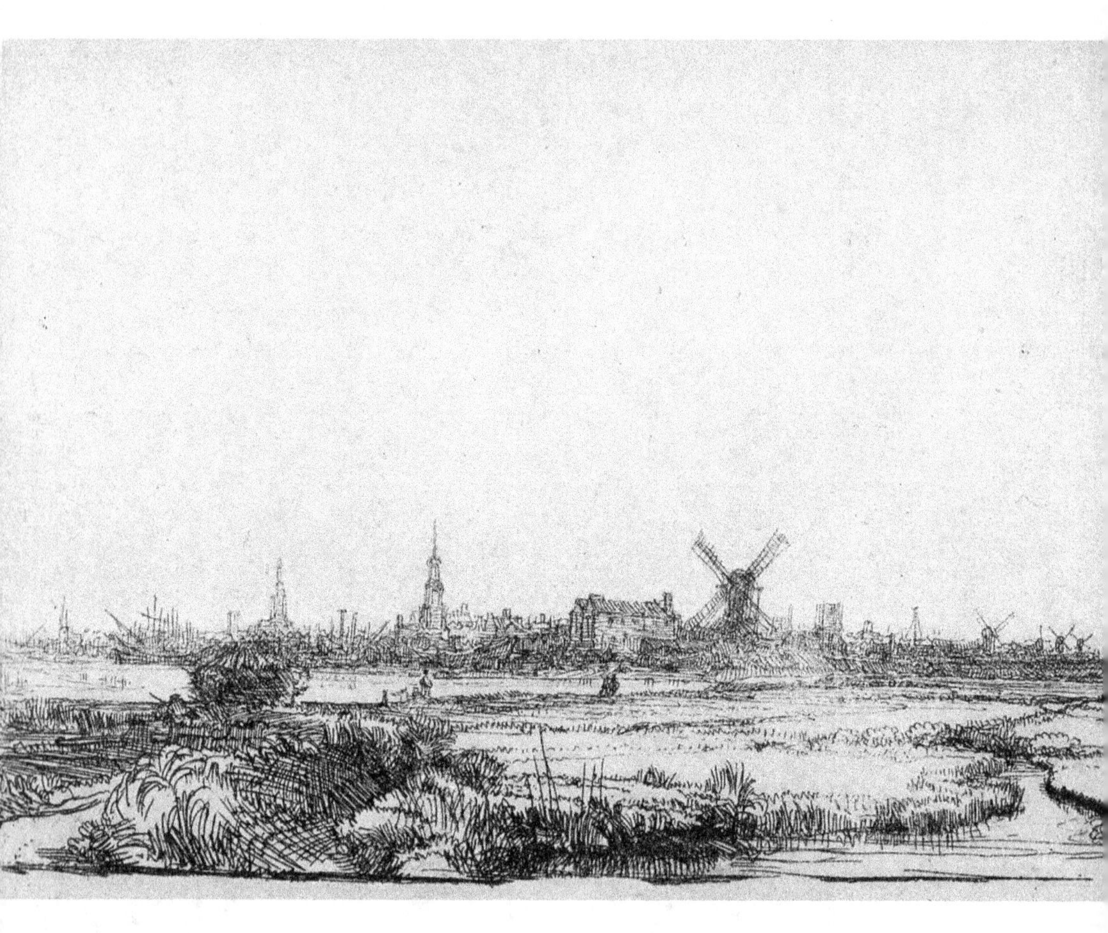

Rembrandt, Amsterdam, c. 1640

# REMBRANDT THE ETCHER

## CHAPTER VIII

## HISTORY OF THE ETCHINGS

We have seen how Rembrandt the painter, after having risen to the foremost place among his fellow-craftsmen in Holland, fell a victim to the always unaccountable change of fashion that has cast a blight upon many another man. Now, however, that we come to consider his etched work, we have, to some extent, a different tale to tell. From the first the products of his needle seem to have been appreciated and sought after, in certain, though perhaps limited, circles. Houbraken mentions Clement de Jonghe, whose shrewd yet kindly face is found among the gallery of portraits etched by Rembrandt, Jan Pietersen Zoomer, and Pieter de la Tombe, as having made collections of his etchings; and in the inventory of the property left by the first of these at his death, on February 11th, 1679, we find a list of seventy-four plates etched by Rembrandt; but it is not therefore to be hastily concluded that Rembrandt himself ever made any important addition to his income by the sale of them.

Indeed, the chief foundation of the belief can be shown to be frail and untrustworthy. This is the familiar title of the etching, "Christ healing the Sick," which has been known for many years as "The Hundred Guilder Print," that having been, according to the story, the sum the artist obtained for a single proof. The amount, even if he had obtained it, was hardly excessive – some nine pounds; but the facts show clearly that he never did. He exchanged a copy, still in existence, with his friend Jan Zoomer, who has left in writing on the back of it, "Given me by my intimate friend Rembrandt in exchange for 'The Pest' of M. Anthony," to which he may possibly have attached the value of a hundred guilders, though there is not a particle of evidence for even this. Gersaint, when making the catalogue, published in 1751, after his death, by Helle and Glomy, was informed that the famous proof was exchanged with a Roman merchant, and the equivalent, like Falstaff s men in buckram, had swelled to seven engravings, which were definitely valued at one hundred guilders; and thence the tradition and the name arose. What, one wonders, would the gossips, who gasped amazed at such a price, have thought could some seer have succeeded in making them believe that, little more than a hundred years later, in 1858, that very same proof with old Jan Zoomer's writing still upon it would be competed for so fiercely at public auction, that M. Dutuit paid cheerfully for it eleven hundred pounds; while even that was not a record price, since another copy was sold the year before at the Palmer sale for eleven hundred and eighty.

Still, though this piece of evidence must be abandoned, there would seem to be no doubt that the etchings were admired even in his lifetime, and, from the fact that Clement de Jonghe and Zoomer were art-dealers, we may fairly conclude that part at least of their collections appertained to their stock-in-trade. It is scarcely probable, indeed, that such highly-finished works as the larger "Raising of Lazarus," "Christ healing the Sick," "Christ preaching," "The Three Crosses," "The Good Samaritan," "The Three Trees," and others, landscapes in especial, were carried out without any subsequent attempts on Rembrandt's part to profit by them; and there is good reason for supposing that the portraits of Jan Uijtenbogaerd and Jan Cornelis Sylvius with their inscriptions and laudatory verses, were intended for sale among the followers and admirers of the two eminent ministers; but the fact remains that we can only assert with any confidence that two out of all the etchings were expressly made for publication, "The Descent from the Cross," and the "Ecce Homo," and neither of these, though signed by Rembrandt "cum privilegio," as issuing from his studio, and executed under his directions, according to the custom of the day, was worked upon by him to any great extent.

The numerous other portraits, the four illustrations to Manasseh ben Israel's work, *Piedra Gloriosa*, and that to *Der Zeeværts-Lof*, were doubtless commissions, but the payments were probably not large, since we found in the proposal made by Dirck van Cattenburch, in 1654, that an etched plate "not less finished than that of Six," was estimated at no more than four hundred florins, which, considering the amount of work entailed, was not magnificent.

When we have recalled the partnership formally entered into between Hendrickje and Titus on December 15, 1660, which has already been explained in telling the story of the artist's life, we have come to the end of the reasons for concluding that the artist made money by his etching needle.

Whence, then, it may be asked, the various proofs now in existence, the first and second, third and fourth states for which collectors pay such surprising prices, prices more often regulated by the rarity of the state than by its special artistic merits? Perhaps some of them were put into circulation by the firm of Hendrickje and Titus. There is, certainly, no mention of the plates in the inventory of the sale, and it is therefore possible that this pathetic little association for the support of a broken-down artist may have found it profitable in a small way to issue new impressions of these earlier completed plates, though it is significant in this connection, unless we can accept the theory suggested before, that

Rembrandt's eyesight was failing, that at the very time when etchings were most needed he ceased to produce them.

In a very large number of cases, I suspect, they were given as presents to any sympathetic soul who had enough taste to appreciate them for their merits, or intelligence enough to foresee that they might some day prove of value. In the case of a portrait, at any rate, we know that he gave proofs to his sitter as the work went on, for on one of the first portrait of Sylvius, done in 1634, there is a note in Rembrandt's hand showing that it was one of four presented by him to the minister.

Others, again, would be given to fellow-artists, such as Lievensz, who etched also. Many undoubtedly came from the sixty portfolios of leather, which we find recorded in the inventory, where they had lain from the day when Rembrandt, having learnt the lesson or attained the effect he desired, had flung them carelessly aside to go on to some further problem. For, there seems little doubt that he never himself regarded them with any very serious consideration. They were for him only steps in his onward progress. He did them because he wanted to do them, without any thoughts of fame or profit, and he signed and dated them, or left them unsigned and undated, in the most haphazard and capricious way, good and bad alike, with the most complete indifference as to whether they were calculated to enhance his reputation or not. It was, therefore, by the inevitable irony of fate, that for these alone, for many years, was he judged worthy of remark. While Gerard de Lairesse in his *Groote Schilderboek*, published in 1714, was condescendingly assuring a listening public that Rembrandt's paintings were not "absolutely bad," Houbraken was recording the struggles of collectors to get possession of his etchings, and their consequent increase in price – struggles and increasings, which have gone on augmenting without intermission to the present day, until even a small representative collection of them is a luxury for the very rich alone, an absolutely perfect one of all the differing states unobtainable by a many times millionaire.

In the eighteenth century there were already famous collections of the etchings: such as those of de Burgy and van Leyden in Holland itself; of Marolles, Coypel, Silvestre, and Mariette in France; of Barnard, Sloane, Cracherode, Fawkener, and Lord Aylesford in England; and it was inevitable that the making of collections could not go on satisfactorily for long, unless there was some sort of general agreement as to what was and what was not to be included in them, so that before long the need for some catalogue to establish at any rate the preliminary basis of an agreement on disputed points became an absolute necessity.

Gersaint was the first to make the attempt, but died before his task was finished. His manuscript, however, was put up for sale, and bought by les Sieurs Helle and Glomy, as they call themselves upon the title-page of the volume in duodecimo which, after making the "necessary augmentations" of Gersaint's material, they published at Paris in 1751. An English translation of this was published by T. Jefferys in London the following year, and four years later, in 1756, Pierre Yver, an art-dealer in Amsterdam, published in that city a "Supplément," with additions and corrections. Forty years later these two works, collated and again translated into English, were the foundation of an amended catalogue by Daniel Daulby, published in London and Liverpool in 1796. A year later Adam Bartsch, keeper of the prints in the Library at Vienna, published there a catalogue in two octavo volumes, which to this day remains the chief standard of appeal, though Wilson, Charles Blanc, Vosmaer, Middleton, and others, have rejected some of the etchings which he accepted, and included others which he ignored.

There is no doubt that Bartsch was too generous in his admissions, but to what extent he carried his over-generosity is still a matter of dispute. The Chevalier de Claussin, writing in 1824, and borrowing freely, though without acknowledgment, from Bartsch, struck out 10, leaving 365; and Wilson, publishing in London in 1836, under the title of "an amateur," while owning his obligations to Bartsch, rejected 6, but added others, making

369. Vosmaer, in 1877, counted 353; Middleton, in the following year, reduced these to 329; Charles Blanc, in the 1880 edition of his work, raised the number again to 353. M. de Seidlitz, in 1890, obtained and collated the opinions of all the best living authorities, and, after an ample discussion of doubtful points, accepted 260; while M. Legros, adopting heroic methods of criticism, will only admit 71 as being certainly by Rembrandt, with an additional 42 which might be, or 113 at the most.

What, it may well be asked by the bewildered amateur, is the reason of these surprising differences? Surely, he may well say, there must be some criterion to hold by. The answer is simple, if unsatisfactory: there is not, there never has been, there never can be. There is no style to judge by; for Rembrandt had half-a-dozen styles at least, and employed them all together or separately as he listed. The signature is no guide, for many beautiful works of his have none, and many that are not his bear forged ones. The subject cannot help us, for he treated alike the most sacred incidents and the grossest improprieties. The merit of the work is no less dubious ground for judgment; for while producing, over and over again, masterpieces of the art that have never been equalled, he at other times, through carelessness, indifference, or perhaps ill-health, turned out and left for future ages stuff which most far inferior men would have obliterated there and then. We can only decide each for ourselves that such or such a plate is in no way worthy of Rembrandt, but, unless we have the courage of M. Legros, we cannot go on to assert definitely that therefore it is not his.

# CHAPTER IX

# THE AUTHENTIC ETCHINGS

In the entire absence of any evidence to the contrary, we are reasonably safe in concluding that the two etchings dated 1628 were, if not actually the first, among the very first he ever did; and, regarded in this light, they are truly astonishing. Both are called Rembrandt's mother, though the one in full face (B. 352) seems to represent a woman in a much humbler station of life than the stately old lady in the other (B. 354), while both, furthermore, seem to portray a woman much more advanced in years than his mother was at that time.

In the first the kindly old lady, whoever she may be, wears a large white hood shading her forehead. The right side of her face, with the exception of the prominence of the cheekbone, is in shadow, and the strong light falling on the left side of the head brings into relief the wrinkles by the nose and at the corner of the mouth, and the soft fleshy forms of the cheek and jaw. The seemingly toothless mouth is slightly open above the strong square chin. The work is simple and straightforward, but admirably expressive of the varied forms, and the roundness and solidity of the little head are excellent. The second (B. 354) is slighter and broader in handling, the forms are expressed with greater freedom, the elaboration of the modelling in the one being often replaced by a single significant line, but the shadows are somewhat forced, which results, especially in the hollow of the cheek and on the right temple, in an excessive and unpleasant blackness. Yet the dash and surety of the line-work is very fine, and to the student it is well worth careful study through a lens. The first excels in delicacy, the second in strength.

The only etching actually known to have been executed in 1629 is the first of many portraits of himself (B. 338), very broadly and strongly etched, and worked upon in places with two needles fastened side by side, a useless device, to which he never again resorted. There are fifteen dated etchings of the year 1630. Among these are no less than six portraits or studies of himself, including an excellent "Portrait in a fur cap and light dress" (B. 24), and an admirably etched study of expression known as "Rembrandt with haggard eyes" (B. 320), which is, rather, a humorous sketch of amazed bewilderment. He also, for the first time, attempted a composition with several figures – "The Presentation in the Temple" (B. 51), distinguished as the one with the angel, which, however, was not altogether a success, owing to insufficient biting. A spirited note of "An Old Beggar Man conversing with a Woman" (B. 164), and various small heads, including two profiles of the same "Bald Man" (B. 292 and 294), which M. Michel has given sound reasons for believing to be Rembrandt's father, make up the number.

He was again his own model twice in 1631 – one, with a broad hat and mantle (B. 7), being the most elaborately finished piece of work he had yet attempted. There are also two "Portraits of his Mother" (B. 348 and 349); one said to be "His Father" (B. 263) though made after his death; a brilliant little sketch of a "Blind Fiddler" (B. 138), and others. There are only three dated etchings of 1632 – a little figure called "The Persian" (B. 152), the first of several pictures of "St Jerome" (B. 101), a subject which had a singular fascination for the artist, and the group of "The Rat-killer" (B. 121). Three also bear the date 1633, "An Old Woman" etched no lower than the chin (B. 351), very doubtfully identified as his mother; a badly overbitten "Portrait of Himself" with a scarf round his neck (B. 17); and one subject, "The Descent from the Cross" (B. 81), which came so utterly to grief in the biting, owing apparently to bad grounding, that it was at once abandoned, only three impressions being known, and a second undertaken, though not by himself, the work having been carried out under his supervision by some unknown pupil. Another equally important plate bearing this date, "The Good Samaritan" (B. 90), is included among the disputed etchings.

The year 1634, which brought Saskia into his home, also naturally enough brought her portrait into the list of etchings. One, with pearls in her hair (B. 347), is certainly a likeness of her, and M. Michel believes it to have been the companion plate to one of Rembrandt (B. 2), executed about the same time. Another charming piece of work, "A Young Woman Reading" (B. 345), though not a portrait, was also very possibly studied from Saskia. For subjects both the Old and New Testaments supplied inspiration, the first for a decidedly seventeenth-century Dutch rendering of "Joseph and Potiphar's Wife" (B. 39), the second for the earliest treatment of a favourite subject "Christ and the Disciples at Emmaus" (B. 88). "Christ driving the Money-lenders from the Temple" (B. 69), a crowded and unsatisfactory composition, the central figure of which was borrowed from Durer; the "Martyrdom of St Stephen" (B. 97), with some singularly bad drawing in it; and another, "St Jerome" (B. 102), were the subjects treated in 1635, which is more notable for a vivacious "Portrait of Johannes Uijtenbogaerd" (B. 279); a splendid little study of "A Mountebank" (B. 129), a model of direct etching from nature wherein there is not a superfluous line, though everything that should be is expressed; and a skilful piece of chiaroscuro, "The Pancake Woman" (B. 124).

1636 has only four etchings to show – "The Prodigal Son" (B. 91), a boldly-handled piece of work, superbly executed, full of movement and expression, but marred by the revolting hideousness of the faces; the excellent portrait of "Manasseh ben Israel" (B. 269); a charming little revelation of domestic contentment, "Rembrandt and his Wife" (B. 19); and a sheet of sketches, including a very pleasing head of Saskia (B. 365). 1637 has only one etching of importance, "Abraham dismissing Hagar" (B. 30); but for sheer skill in craftsmanship the "Young Man seated in Meditation" (B. 268) would be difficult to match.

Rembrandt's unfortunate lack of the sense of beauty is nowhere so glaringly made manifest as in the preposterous "Adam and Eve" (B. 28) of 1638; nor are the faces in an etching of that year, rejected, however, by Sir Seymour Haden, of the brothers listening to "Joseph relating His Dreams" (B. 37) much less absurd, though they are to a considerable extent atoned for by the dignified Jacob, the very human interest of Rachel, and the simple earnestness of Joseph himself. The "St Catherine," otherwise known as "The Little Jewish Bride" (B. 342), and a "Portrait of Himself with a Mezetin Cap and Feather" (B. 20), are the only others of the year. In the following year he achieved, with conspicuous success, the most ambitious etching he had yet attempted, the magnificent "Death of the Virgin" (B. 99), which, with the exception of the unfortunate angels hovering above, is admirable alike in conception and execution, attaining by straightforward simplicity the full pathos of the scene. The truthfulness and variety of attitude and expression, the wholly effective yet unforced arrangement of the composition, and the perfection of the chiaroscuro are beyond praise, and justify the somewhat bold assertion that beyond this the etcher's art cannot go. It is no matter for wonder, therefore, that this splendid plate seems to have absorbed most of the time he could devote to etching that year, for a little sketch of "A Jew in a High Cap" (B. 133), and the fine "Portrait of Himself leaning on a Stone Sill" (B. 21), alone share the date with it. His interest or his leisure would indeed appear to have been exhausted for some time, since only two small etchings, "The Beheading of St John the Baptist" (B. 92), and "An Old Man with a divided Fur Cap" (B. 265), are dated

1640.

A return of energy, however, marked 1641, from which year we have twelve dated plates; among them, the first three, to our certain knowledge, of a long series of landscapes, the elaborate study known as "Rembrandt's Mill" (B. 233), the beautiful "Cottage and Barn" (B. 225), and the "Landscape with a Cottage and Mill Sail" (B. 226). There are four subjects from scripture – a "Virgin and Child in the Clouds" (B. 61), "The Baptism of the Eunuch" (B. 98), one called "Jacob and Laban" (B. 118), and "The Angel departing from Tobit and his Family" (B. 43), in which his inability to perceive the absurd and undignified is once again demonstrated in the inflated petticoat and foreshortened legs which are all that is seen of the angel. A little night-effect, "The Schoolmaster" (B. 128), and the grand and very rare "Portrait of Anslo" (B. 271), are the most important of the remainder. With the exception of a "Bearded Man seated at a Table in an Arbour" (B. 257), the only etchings of 1642 were three sacred subjects, all small, and two of them, "The Raising of Lazarus" (B. 72) and "The Descent from the Cross" (B. 82), mere sketches. The finished plate represents "St Jerome" (B. 105), distinguished as being in Rembrandt's dark manner, seated reading at a table in a room lighted only by one window high up in front of him, so that the contrasts of light and shade are strong, and the effect very excellent.

1643 has only two signed etchings, but both are masterpieces of out-door work – "The Hog" (B. 157), and the justly-renowned "Three Trees" (B. 212). There is only one etching dated 1644, a landscape with figures, called "The Shepherd and his Family" (B. 220).

A superb combination of pure etching and dry-point dates from 1645 – the "View of Omval, near Amsterdam" (B. 209), one of the most entirely satisfactory of the etchings, both for perfection of workmanship and beauty of effect. The transition from the loving care bestowed upon the splendid study of the gnarled and shattered willow-tree in front, through the more broadly yet quite adequately expressed foliage behind it on the left, to the slight yet all-sufficient treatment of the river and landscape beyond it on the right, shows a precise adaptation of the necessary means to the desired end, which, had no other line of Rembrandt's etching come down to us, would have been enough to stamp him as the finest known exponent of the art. A second landscape of that year is a study of a boat-house, known as "The Grotto" (B. 231); and a third, the one known as "Six's Bridge" (B. 208), a masterly little sketch from nature. As an example of the utmost expressiveness with the fewest necessary means, of a thorough grasp of the essentials and rejection of superfluities, and of a profound mastery of technical methods, this etching cannot easily be over-estimated. An outline sketch of the "Repose in Egypt" (B. 58), and a more highly finished "Abraham conversing with Isaac" just previous to the projected sacrifice (B. 34), are the only subject-etchings of that year, which is further remarkable for the absence of any portraits or studies of heads.

The next few years are singularly devoid of dated etchings. There are three from 1646 – a small sketch of "An Old Beggar Woman" (B. 170); a subject known as "Ledikant" (B. 186), one of those frank improprieties to the perpetration of which Rembrandt, with the freedom of his time, more than once degraded his talents, from our modern point of view; and a direct study from the nude model, "A Man seated on the Ground" (B. 196). 1647 has only two, both highly-finished endeavours to realise a wholly pictorial effect – an endeavour which, however successful, is always to some extent a mis-application of the art, a deliberate sacrifice of its special advantages, in order to attain an object more easily and efficiently obtainable in other ways. Still, regarded as attempts to express the full tonality, there is much to admire and study in these two portraits of "Six" (B. 285), and "Ephraim Bonus" (B. 278), the Jewish physician, descending a staircase, with his right hand on the banister, as if pausing on his return from visiting a patient, a reversed reproduction of the picture in the Six collection already referred to.

In 1648 he once more undertook a "Portrait of Himself" (B. 22), a very different presentment from the earlier ones, with their feathered caps and embroidered cloaks, their flowing locks and brushed up moustaches. Time and trouble have told upon him, and it is pathetic to contrast the proud elegance of the Rembrandt of 1639 (B. 21), his fine clothes, rich velvet cap flung carelessly on one side of his long curling hair, and his self-satisfied air, with this grave, soberly-clad, middle-aged man, in his plain, high, square-topped, broad-brimmed hat, and dark working blouse. His cavalier curls are cropped, his once airily upturned moustache trimmed short, the dainty tuft upon his chin is gone. He has grown stout, his throat hangs in puffy folds below his chin, his nose has coarsened, and he bears his two-and-forty years but badly; but if his face has aged, it has also strengthened, he has learned as well as suffered, and, if there is no longer in his eyes the look of undoubting self-approval, there is still the same keen, penetrating gaze of observation, and a wiser self-confidence born of trials and labours past and overcome. Among all the portraits of Rembrandt, real or supposed, there is none which makes one feel so strongly that here, indeed, one is face to face with him, as he saw himself when he sat drawing from the mirror in front of him.

Another splendid example of that year is the "Beggars at the Door of a House" (B. 176), a masterpiece of composition and workmanship. It has all the rich effect of a highly-laboured piece of work, yet a careful study of it shows how simple and direct are the means actually employed; for the elaborately-finished effect, it will be found, is due, not to the multiplication of lines, but to the absolute rightness and appropriateness of the comparatively few that are used. The crispness and firmness of the drawing are quite magnificent, and it is satisfactory to know that this marvellous little plate, simple and unsensational as it is, comes third, according to M. Amand Durand, in popularity with the purchasers of reproductions. Yet another masterpiece of the same year is "The Jews' Synagogue" (B. 126); and a fourth etching is "The Marriage of Jason and Creusa" (B. 112), a composition of many figures, made to illustrate his friend Jan Six's tragedy of Medea, published that year, in which, as usual with him, the attempt to convey the classical spirit was scarcely successful.

There is no etching which we can definitely assign to 1649. In 1650, on the other hand, we have six, including four landscapes, to which he again turned his attention after an interval of five years. These are "A Village by the High-Road" (B. 217), with its big tree and high-gabled cottages; the excellent "Village with a Square Tower" (B. 218); the "Canal with Swans" (B. 235); and the sketch of "A Canal with a Large Boat" (B. 236) lying broadside on athwart the foreground, which is, however, chiefly interesting from the background, which has given rise to a question as to whether Rembrandt was about that time on his travels to some place unknown. This hilly distance, with the steep cliff on the left, and the Italian-looking tower in the centre, certainly bears no resemblance to anything in his ordinary surroundings, but there is nothing in it to assure us that it was done from nature, and as we know that he more than once adapted a landscape from some Italian master, generally Titian, it would be rash to found any conclusion on the resemblance.

A remarkable instance of patient and loving care is seen in the "Shell" (B. 159), an astonishingly truthful and minute study of still life, which is equally attractive in the first state against a plain white background, and in the second against a nearly black one, which, however, may have been added by some other hand. The sixth etching of that year, "Christ appearing to the Disciples" (B. 89), is a sketch in outline with a little tentative shading here and there, and, though handled with freedom and boldness, has little of interest or beauty to recommend it.

During 1651 he devoted himself once and once only to each class of work; for there is one subject, "The Flight into Egypt" (B. 53), showing Joseph carrying a lantern, and leading the ass bearing the Virgin and Child through the night; one landscape, "The Goldweigher's Field" (B. 234) – so called from the view including the country-house of his friend Uijtenbogaerd, the treasurer, whose portrait, etched by Rembrandt, is known as "The Goldweigher"; and one portrait, "Clement de Jonghe" (B. 272), one of the best, if not the best, he ever did. Still fewer etchings were produced in 1652, and one of the two, the larger "Christ disputing with the Doctors" (B. 65), is only a sketch – in places, indeed, it degenerates to a mere scrawl – displaying, for Rembrandt, an unwonted amount of indifferent and inexpressive drawing; but the other, a landscape, generally known in England as the "Vista" (B. 222), with the two large trees on the left and the dense wood in the centre, is, perhaps, the finest specimen of work in pure dry-point ever produced.

1653 is, again, a blank as far as dated etchings are concerned, but to 1654 belong eight, seven of which are subjects from the New Testament; a "Circumcision" (B. 47), known as the one with the cask and net; a sketch of "The Holy Family crossing a Rill during the Flight into Egypt" (B. 55), in which the figures are clumsily and unpleasantly thrown into relief by a band of shadow closely following their outlines in very naïve fashion, but which, nevertheless, contains a great deal of bold and expressive drawing; "Jesus and His Parents returning from Jerusalem" (B. 60), in which we have another instance of an altogether foreign landscape, which might as well be adduced in evidence of his foreign travels as that of four years before. In this case, however, it has evidently been so closely copied from an unknown original that there can be no doubt that there is somewhere, or at any rate was then, a drawing of the subject, and there is, furthermore, a very high degree of probability that the drawing was by Titian. The figures are full of movement, and there is, in especial, much animation in the young Christ, who, led by His father, himself leads His mother, turning half backwards as He walks to speak to her, but the types of the heads, especially that of the Virgin Mary, are disagreeably ugly and vulgar. The Virgin in "The Holy Family with the Serpent" (B. 63), has, on the other hand, an unusual amount of grace, but this, it has to be admitted, is due to the fact that it is borrowed from Mantegna, and the plate is otherwise an indifferent piece of work. "Christ and the Disciples at Emmaus" (B. 87) is, again, no more than a sketch, presenting with much vividness the actions of surprise on the part of the two disciples and of the serving-man descending the stairs in front; but here, as so often elsewhere, Rembrandt has failed to rise to any sense of the sublimity or dignity of Christ, and as, in this example, he sits in full face in the very centre of the picture, the fault cannot well be overlooked or condoned. A far more satisfactory production, indeed the best of the year, is "The Descent from the Cross by Torchlight" (B. 83), with its bold drawing and coarse yet effective handling, but, like all the work of 1654, it has serious and obvious defects; while the last to be noted, "The Game of Golf" or Kolf (B. 125), is yet another instance of Rembrandt's contentedly signing a work which would disgrace a man without a tithe of his genius, and is one of those plates which, if it be authentic – and no one else that I know of disputes it – renders any test of genuineness by workmanship impossible.

1655 saw Rembrandt employed once more as an illustrator, the book being one entitled "Piedra gloriosa ò de la estatua de Nebucadnezar," by his friend Manasseh ben Israel, for which he etched four subjects on one plate, afterwards sub-divided – "Jacob's Dream," "The Combat of David and Goliath," "Nebuchadnezzar's Dream," and "The Vision of Ezekiel" (B. 36). "Abraham's Sacrifice" (B. 35), of the same year, is another of those bold and rapid sketches in which Rembrandt seems to have dashed at his subject and realised it by sheer force of energy, caring little about detail, shading where he wanted shadows, and omitting them where he wanted light, without any regard to where light and shade would have been, yet putting such vitality, such genuine, undeniable, human feeling into it, that even bad drawing passes unnoticed. The swirl of the broad-winged angel swooping down from behind on Abraham, grasping his left arm just above he elbow to hold back the knife, while with his right he removes Abraham's right hand from the eyes of the resignedly kneeling Isaac, is marvellous. The startled surprise of Abraham is amazingly true; and, carried away by the vigour of the actions and the sound breadth of the work, we ignore the fact that Abraham is left-handed, and that the angel has no forearm. Another equally bold work in outline is "Christ before Pilate" (B. 76), with its wonderful crowd of figures in the foreground relieved against the platform on which Christ and Pilate stand surrounded by soldiers. The only highly-finished work of the year is the "Portrait of Thomas Jacobsz Haring" (B. 275), known as "The Young Haring," to distinguish it from the etching of his father "The Old Haring."

There are only two etchings dated 1656, – "Abraham entertaining the Angels" (B. 29), in which yet again we have forced upon us the incapacity of Rembrandt's mind to evolve an acceptable supernatural figure, and the splendid "Portrait of Jan Lutma" (B. 276). It is impossible to look on this and doubt that it is an admirable likeness of a delightful old man. With what a shrewd humorous expression he sits in that high-backed arm-chair, surmounted by lions' heads, which figures in so many of Rembrandt's portraits at that time. How broad and easy, yet neither over-laboured nor careless, is the handling. Rembrandt never worked better, and one cannot but feel convinced, in regarding the result, that, to both artist and sitter, the work was a labour of love, and the sittings periods of mutual enjoyment. In this, the last dated portrait we have, he reached the highest pitch of excellence he ever attained.

In 1657, as far as we know, he executed only one etching, "St Francis praying" (B. 107), unfinished, and chiefly notable for the fine study of a tree which it contains. Three figures of nude women, "A Woman preparing to dress after Bathing" (B. 199), "A Woman sitting with her Feet in Water" (B. 200), and a so-called "Negress lying down" (B. 205), are dated 1658, while 1659 was marked by two very diverse subjects, "St Peter and St John at the Gate of the Temple" (B. 94), and "Jupiter disguised as a Satyr discovering the sleeping Antiope" (B. 203).

Throughout 1660 Rembrandt would seem to have left his

etching needle to rust in idleness, but he resumed it once more in 1661, and produced a study of the nude, "A Woman with her Back turned sitting cross-legged upon a Bed, holding an Arrow in her right Hand" (B. 202); and with this the list of authentic dated etchings is brought to a close.

There are one hundred and one etchings generally accepted as Rembrandt's to which no date can positively be assigned, but lack of space forbids our considering them at length, and we must be content to review them somewhat hastily, dwelling only on those of special importance. The earlier years, from 1628 or 1629 to about 1635, are chiefly characterised by a number of small portraits of himself, and of various unknown old men and old women, and by a remarkable series of sketches of beggars and peasants. About 1631 we find the first study from the nude, "Diana bathing" (B. 201), altogether excellent as an example of well-directed line, devoted, however, to a coarse and unshapely figure. Of approximately the same date is a masterly portrait of "An Old Lady," in all probability Rembrandt's mother (B. 343), seated at a table, turned in three-quarter face to the right, her hands lightly folded in her lap, which is worthy of remark as showing how rapidly Rembrandt mastered all the available styles of etching, and how subtly and skilfully he combined them.

A little later, the assigned dates ranging between 1633 and 1636, we have the first portrait, outside his family circle, to which we can definitely attach a name, that of the minister "Jan Cornelis Sylvius" (B. 266), with whose family Saskia was staying before her marriage. If, as we may imagine, it was undertaken to ingratiate himself with people so important to him, or later out of gratitude for their good offices, we can only hope that they were not over-critical, for it must be confessed that this exercise in pure dry-point is about as bad an example as could be found. A sheet of sketches (B. 367), dating from 1635 or 1636, is noteworthy for the charming "Head of Saskia" included in it, and a "Portrait of Himself in a flat cap and slashed vest" (B. 26), slightly but beautifully etched, as undoubtedly an admirable presentment of himself as he appeared about 1638. Four scripture subjects are, a sketch of "The Flight into Egypt" (B. 54), dating anywhere between 1630 and 1640; a "Holy Family," known as "The Virgin with the Linen" (B. 62), dating between 1632 and 1640; a beautiful little "Crucifixion" (B. 80), dating from 1634 or 1635; and "An Old Man caressing a Boy," who stands between his knees (B. 33), dating from 1638 or 1639, believed by some authorities to represent "Abraham caressing Isaac."

There are, altogether, forty-eight etchings attributed with every probability of correctness to the years before 1640, many of which deserve more attention than we can spare them; while two, "A Sketch of a Tree" (B. 372), and "The Presentation in the vaulted Temple" (B. 49), are placed by some a year or two earlier, by others a year or two later, than that year. To the year itself probably belongs a landscape "A large Tree by a House" (B. 207), and to it or to the following year "The Virgin mourning the Death of Jesus" (B. 85), "The Flute-Player" (B. 188), and "A View of Amsterdam" (B. 210); while to 1641 are generally assigned two sketches of lion-hunts (B. 115 and 116), more remarkable for energy of action then accuracy of drawing; a vigorous "Battle-Scene" (B. 117); "The Draughtsman" (B. 130), and "A Portrait of a Boy" (B. 310). Other landscapes, of doubtful date, but almost certainly of some year between 1640 and 1650, are, "The Bull" (B. 253), "A Village with a River and Sailing Vessel" (B. 228), the beautiful "Landscape with a Man sketching" (B. 219), and the "Landscape with a ruined Tower" (B. 223). Portraits of known originals are those of "Jan Asselyn" (B. 277), a fellow-artist, a dwarfed, deformed little man, nicknamed by his contemporaries the little Crab, whose personal failings evidently did not weigh on him, for he stands gazing at the spectator with a superb air of ludicrous conceit; and a magnificent one of the same "Jan Sylvius" (B. 280) with whom Rembrandt had so conspicuously failed before, so full of life and movement that it is hard to believe, though an indubitable fact, that it was etched from a study in 1645 or 1646, seven or eight years after the death of the minister. The scripture subjects of this decade include an oval "Crucifixion" (B. 79), and "The Triumph of Mordecai" (B. 40).

In the debatable land between the late forties and the early fifties there are two magnificent works, one, oddly included in the usual classifications among the portraits, "Dr Faustus" (B. 270), the other the famous Hundred Guilder print, "Jesus Christ healing the Sick" (B. 74). There are, all told, twenty-eight etchings dating between 1640 and 1650.

Only eighteen of uncertain date are placed between 1650 and the end of Rembrandt's career as an etcher in 1661, but they are nearly all worthy of more space than can be devoted to them. One is a landscape, "The Sportsman" (B. 211). Five are portraits, one of "A Youth," long known as Rembrandt, but undoubtedly his son Titus (B. 11); the large one of "Coppenol" (B. 283), probably among the last of the etchings, but beautifully and minutely finished in an exquisitely delicate fashion, though the hands are less well expressed than usual with Rembrandt, who, whether in painting or drawing, delighted in bringing out with care the full character revealed by them; a portrait in dry-point of "Dr Arnoldus Tholinx" (B. 284), of which it would be impossible to speak too highly; a less admirable one of "Abraham Francen" (B. 273), whose long and faithful friendship with the painter has been referred to in the *Life*; and one of Jacob Haring (B. 274), known as "The Old Haring."

There are nine scripture subjects of the period, two from the Old Testament, "King David at Prayer" (B. 41), a strong and unhesitating piece of work, in which, however, the face of the king is somewhat too simply expressed, but was probably not considered by Rembrandt as finished; and "Tobit Blind" (B. 42), scarcely more than a sketch, but full of the sentiment of helpless blindness. Of the seven subjects from the New Testament two are of the first importance, "Christ preaching" (B. 67), known as the little La Tombe, because, it is supposed, the plate came into the possession of the dealer of that name; and the "Three Crosses" (B. 78), the former being an etching heightened by dry-point, the second a work in dry-point throughout. "Jesus Christ entombed" (B. 86) is a powerful and effective etching dating probably from the early fifties, and "The Presentation in the Temple" (B. 50), further identified as being in Rembrandt's dark manner, from about the middle of the decade. "The Nativity" (B. 45), of about the same time, is an exquisite little composition expressed with the utmost simplicity compatible with the desired result. In "Christ in the Garden of Olives" (B. 75), on the other hand, this rapidity of work has been carried too far, and degenerates into sheer carelessness, though, apart from details, the arrangement of the masses of light and shade is good. "Christ and the Samaritan Woman" (B. 70), dating from 1657 or 1658, is drawn with precision and delicacy, but the device of relieving the face of the woman by a dark and impossible shadow on a building in the background, is scarcely a happy or successful one. A figure of "A Nude Woman sitting by a Dutch stove" (B. 197), a portrait of "A Goldsmith at his Work" (B. 123), and "A Sheet of Sketches" (B. 364), of which only three copies are known, bring the tale of etchings to which an approximate date may be assigned to a conclusion.

There remain seventeen, concerning the probable dates of which conjectures vary so widely, that it is safer to admit we do not know, and cannot guess with any prospect of success. Thus the clever little sketch of "Two Beggars walking towards the right" (B. 144), has been dated 1629, 1634, and 1648; another "Beggar leaning upon a Stick" (B. 162), 1631 and 1641, and a pathetic little composition of "Christ's Body carried to the Tomb" (B. 84), 1632 and 1645; while the small "Portrait of Coppenol" (B. 282), has been attributed by one to 1632, but by another to as far away as 1651. Other plates of equally uncertain date are five landscapes – the exquisite "Landscape with a Flock of Sheep" (B. 224), and the no less admirable "Peasant with Milk Pails" (B. 213); "The Cottage with white Pales" (B. 232), "The Canal" (B. 221), the "Landscape with an Obelisque" (B. 227), and the "Landscape with a Cow drinking" (B. 237). Three are scripture subjects – "The Adoration of the Shepherds" (B. 46), a hurriedly executed night effect, dating between 1632 and 1640 according to Vosmaer, from 1652 according to Middleton; a second night effect, "The Repose in Egypt" (B. 57), also assigned by Vosmaer to some date between 1632 and 1640, by M. Michel to 1641 or 1642, and by Middleton to 1647; and a very indifferent "St Peter" (B. 96), with a signature and date which Middleton reads 1645, Vosmaer 1655. Another dated plate is "The Bathers" (B. 195), which, according to M. Michel, was originally dated 1631, the 3 having subsequently been altered by Rembrandt into a 5. As to the why and wherefore of such an incomprehensible error on the artist's part, he offers no conjecture, but that the etching does not, at any rate, belong to the earlier year is indicated by the fact that it is signed Rembrandt in full, while all the certain plates of that year are signed with a monogram, the first to bear the full name being the "St Jerome" (B. 101) of 1632. A third plate bearing a date, concerning the interpretation of which the authorities differ, is the mysterious allegorical one "The Phœnix" (B. 110), Vosmaer and Wilson making it 1648, M. Michel and Middleton 1658; while a fourth, "A Sheet of Sketches with a head of Himself" (B. 370), is dated so indistinctly that it has been read as 1630, 1631, and 1650. As, however, it is signed with a monogram, it certainly belongs to one of the earlier years. "The Star of the Kings" (B. 113), a subject from contemporary life, representing a party of boys carrying a large illuminated star through the streets of a town at Epiphany, dating either from 1641 or 1652, is the last to be mentioned of the undisputed etchings.

DISPUTED ETCHINGS AND DRAWINGS

At the question of the disputed etchings we have not space even to glance. It is a delicate and difficult one, and could only be treated to any advantage at considerable length. It is, furthermore, one of interest to experts and collectors alone, and so directly opposite in many cases are their opinions that it is certain no finality can ever be hoped for. The reader who desires to enter upon this thorny ground must content himself with pinning his faith finally to one or another recognised authority, and abiding by his decision; unless, having first thoroughly studied the undisputed etchings, he is prepared to undertake the trial and judgment of each for himself, in which case he will, without doubt, sooner or later find himself differing on one point or another with every previous writer on the subject.

The less ambitious reader, who wishes only to know and appreciate what Rembrandt beyond question did do, will be wiser to confine himself to a study of the undisputed plates. In them he will find ample justification for the high position to which Rembrandt as an etcher has been elevated by his successors in the art. Beginning with the early etchings of himself or the members of his family, often mere drawings on copper, with little or no appeal to the variety of line and tone obtainable in etching, he may follow the artist's sure and rapid development, until he finds him master of every method the art permits. He may trace the progress of his work, from a first sketch of an idea, dashed off on the copper in one sitting, to the high perfection of such an elaborate portrait as that of "Burgomaster Six." He will further perceive, as was first pointed out by Sir F. Seymour Haden, how during the first ten years he confined himself almost entirely to pure etching, how during the following ten he began more and more to supplement his work with additions in dry-point, and how during the last ten years he to a considerable extent expressed himself by means of the point alone. He will, in especial, discover, if he compares Rembrandt's etched work with that of other masters, and without doing so he can never rightly understand it, that it is not in technique, masterly as that often is, so much as in expressiveness that his pre-eminence lies. It is in the mental qualities more than in the manual, that he so incomparably excels. Drawing often carelessly, blind or indifferent to superficial beauties, he, nevertheless, gets straight to the heart of the matter, grasps the essentials, and feels clearly and records frankly and simply all that speaks to the fundamental humanity in himself, and must therefore strike an answering chord in the breasts of his fellow-men. It is in this perceiving and revealing the true inwardness of the matter, through and apart from the mere accidents of environment, that he is unapproachable, far more than in the strength and direction of line, depth of shadow or brightness of light, application of acid or scraping of copper. In such a plate as the "Blind Tobit" (B. 42) there is not a detail of the technique which other men could not have done as well; but for such another presentment of the hurried, helpless groping for the door by a blind, weak old man not yet inured to the perpetual darkness that has fallen on him, we must wait for a second Rembrandt – and the wait is likely to be long.

Of the drawings I propose to speak very briefly. In the first place, their name is legion, and to treat them properly would take a volume in itself, such a volume as we may hope some day to see written. M. Michel gives a list of nearly nine hundred, which does not pretend to be a full one. The British Museum alone contains ninety authentic drawings and a considerable number of more or less doubtful ones. In the second place, their qualities are such as to appeal almost exclusively to the artist. Rembrandt's impetuous energy did not lend itself to the production of the minute and elegant drawings characteristic of so many Italian masters. He made the drawing for the sake of what it had to tell him, not for the purpose of creating a thing beautiful in itself. An idea crossed his mind, or an object struck his eye, and straightway he jotted it down with whatever came the handiest in the simplest possible manner consistent with the necessity that the note so made should subsequently recall to his memory the idea or object.

Most attractive, perhaps, to the amateur, are the numberless little sketches of landscapes, just the simple everyday scenes that caught his eye during his daily walks, jotted down on the spot, briefly, but with extraordinary truth and vivacity, and always with a sense of balance and proportion, and an intuition of the salient points, transmuted by his own genius into gems of reticent perfection.

# BIBLIOGRAPHY


Amand-Durand. "Œuvre de Rembrandt reproduit et publié par." 2 parts. Paris, 1880.

Baldinucci, Filippo. "Cominciamento e progresso dell' arte dell' intagliare in rame." Florence, 1686.

Bartsch, Adam. "Catalogue raisonné de toutes les estampes qui forment l'œuvre de Rembrandt et ceux de ses principaux imitateurs." 2 vols. Vienna, 1797.

Bell, Malcolm. "Rembrandt van Rijn and his Work." 4to. London, 1899.

Blanc, Charles. "L'œuvre complet de Rembrandt, décrit et commenté par." Paris, 1864 and 1880.

Bode, W. "Studien zur Geschichte der holländischen Malerei." Brunswick, 1883.

Bredius, A., and de Roever, N. *Oud-Holland.* A magazine published at Amsterdam.

Bredius, A. "Les chefs-d'œuvre du Musée royal d'Amsterdam." Paris, 1890.

Bredius, A. "Die Meisterwerke der Königlichen Gemälde Galerie im Haag." Munich, 1890.

Burger, W. "Les Musées de Belgique et de Hollande." Paris, 1858, 1860, and 1862.

Busken-Huet. "Het Land van Rembrandt." Harlem, 1886.

Chalon, John. Works of Rembrandt, etched by. London, 1822.

Claussin, Chevalier de. "Catalogue raisonné de toutes les estampes qui forment l'œuvre de Rembrandt." Paris, 1824.

Claussin, Chevalier de. "Supplément au Catalogue de Rembrandt." Paris, 1828.

Dargenville. "Abrégé de la Vie des plus fameux peintres." Paris, 1745.

Daulby, Daniel. "A descriptive catalogue of the works of Rembrandt and of his scholars." London and Liverpool, 1796.

Descamps. "Vies des peintres flamands et hollandais." Marseilles, 1840.

Dyk, J. van. "Beschryving van alle de Schilderyen op het Stadhuis van Amsterdam." Amsterdam, 1758.

Dutuit, E. "L'œuvre complet de Rembrandt décrit et catalogué par." Paris, 1880.

Eckhoff. "La femme de Rembrandt." 1862.

Félibien. "Entretien sur les Vies et les Ouvrages des plus excellents peintres." 1666-1688.

Fromentin, Eugène. "Les Maitres d'autrefois." Paris, 1877.

Galland, G. "Geschichte der holländischen Baukunst und Bildnerei." Leipzig, 1890.

Gersaint. "Catalogue raisonné de toutes les pièces qui forment l'œuvre de Rembrandt." Paris, 1751.

Hamerton, P. G. "Etching and Etchers." London, 1868.

Hamerton, P. G. Rembrandt's Etchings. Portfolio. London, 1894.

Havard, Henri. "L'art et les artistes hollandais." Paris, 1879.

Hoogstraten, Samuel van. "Inleyding tot de hooge School der Schilderkonst." Rotterdam, 1678.

Houbraken, Arnold. "De groote Schoubourgh der nederlandsche Kontschilders." Amsterdam, 1718-1719.

Humphreys, Noel. Rembrandt's Etchings. London, 1871.

Huygens, Constantin. "Autobiographie inédite." Library of the Academy of Sciences, Amsterdam.

Kolloff, Édouard. "Rembrandt's Leben und Werke," included in *Historisches Taschenbuch* of von Raumer. Leipzig, 1854.

Langbehn, Dr. "Rembrandt als Erzieher." Published anonymously, Leipzig, 1890.

Lemcke, C. Rembrandt van Rijn, in the *Kunst and Künstler*, Leipzig, 1877.

Lippmann, F. Original drawings by Rembrandt reproduced in Phototype. London, Berlin, and Paris, 1889-1892.

Madsen, Karl. "Studier fra Sverig." Copenhagen, 1892.

Michel, Emile. "Rembrandt sa vie, son œuvre et son temps." Paris, 1893.

Middleton, C. H. "Notes on the Etched Work of Rembrandt." London, 1877.

Middleton, C. H. "A descriptive Catalogue of the Etched Work of Rembrandt." London, 1878.

Orlers, J. J. "Beschryving der Stad Leiden." Leyden, 1641.

Oud-Holland. See *Bredius*.

Piles, R. de. "Abrégé de la vie des Peintres." 1699.

Riegel, Herman. "Beitrage zur niederländischen Kunstgeschichte." Berlin,

1882.

Rovinski, Dmitri. "L'œuvre gravé de Rembrandt." Reproductions of all the states of all the etchings. St. Petersburg, 1890.

Sandrart, Joachim de. "Academia nobilissimae artis pictoriæ." Nuremberg, 1675-1683.

Scheltema, Dr. "Rembrandt, Discours sur sa vie et son génie." Paris, 1866.

Schmidt, W. "Handzeichnungen alter Meister in Königlichen Kupferstich Kabinet zu Munchen. Munich.

Schneider, L. "Geschichte der niederländischen Litteratur." Leipzig, 1888.

Seidlitz, von. "Rembrandt's Radirungen." Published in Zeitschrift für bildende Kunst. 1892.

Seymour Haden, Sir Francis. "Introductory Remarks to the Catalogue of the Etched Work of Rembrandt, selected for exhibition at the Burlington Fine Arts Club, London, 1877."

Seymour Haden, Sir Francis. "L'œuvre gravé de Rembrandt." Paris, 1880.

Seymour Haden, Sir Francis. "The Etched Work of Rembrandt, True and False." London, 1895.

Smith, John. "Catalogue raisonné of the Works of the most eminent Dutch, Flemish, and French Painters." London, 1829-1842.

Springer, Anton. "Bilder aus der neueren Kunstgeschichte. Vol. II. Rembrandt und seine Genossen." Bonn, 1886.

Vosmaer, Charles. "Rembrandt Hermannsz. Sa vie et ses œuvres." Paris and the Hague, 1877.

Weyerman, J. Campo. "De Levens Beschryvingen der nederlandsche Konstschilders." The Hague, 1749.

Willigen, van der. "Les artistes de Harlem." 1870.

Willshire, W. H. "An Introduction to the Study and Collection of Ancient Prints." London, 1877.

Wilson, T. A Descriptive Catalogue of the Prints of Rembrandt. Published as by "An amateur." London, 1836.

Woltmann, A., and Woermann, K. "Geschichte de Malerei." Leipzig.

Yver, Pierre. "Supplément au Catalogue raisonné de MM. Gersaint, Helle, et Glomy." Amsterdam, 1756.

# CATALOGUE OF WORKS

ARRANGED ACCORDING TO THE GALLERIES IN WHICH THEY HANG

*The following abbreviations are used in this list. – S. = signed, C. = canvas, P. = panel.*

*Where a number is given, thus [No. 6], it is the number of the Catalogue of the Gallery. The dates given must in some cases be accepted as approximate only.*

AUSTRIA-HUNGARY

BUDA-PESTH, ACADEMY.
Portrait of an Old Man with a white beard. S. 1640. P. [No. 235.]
Repose of the Holy Family. 1655.

COLLECTION OF COUNT J. ANDRASSY.
Portrait of Himself. S. 1630. P.

COLLECTION OF MR GEORGE VON RATH.
Mountain Landscape. S. 1638. P.
Slaughtered Ox. S. 1639. P.
Portrait of a Woman. S. 1660. P.

CRACOW, CZARTORYSKI MUSEUM.
Landscape. S. 1638. P.

INNSBRUCK, FERDINANDEUM.
Head of an Old Man. S. 1630. P.

PRAGUE. COUNT NOSTITZ.
An Old Man. S. 1634. C. [No. 269.]

TARNOWITZ, GALICIA. COUNT TARNOWSKI.
Polish Horseman. 1655. C.

VIENNA, ACADEMY.
Portrait of a Young Woman. S. 1632. C.

COUNT KÖNIGSWARTER.
Portrait of Rembrandt. S. 1640. C.

PRINCE LIECHTENSTEIN.
Portrait of Saskia. S. 1632. P.
Young Girl at her Toilet, called the Jewish fiancée. S. 1632. C.
Portrait of Rembrandt. S. 1635. C.
Portrait of a Man. S. 1636.
Portrait of a Woman. Companion to above. S. 1636.

PRINCE LUBOMIRSKI.
Study of Rembrandt with his Mouth open. 1629. P.

FRANZ XAVIER MEYER.
A Philosopher reading by Candlelight. 1627. Copper. A very doubtful
picture.

IMPERIAL MUSEUM.
Portrait of a Man. 1630. P. [No. 1139.]
Portrait of a Woman. P. [No. 1140.]
St Paul. 1636. C.
Portrait of Rembrandt's Mother. S. 1639. P. [No. 1141.]
Portrait of Himself. 1658. C. [No. 1142.]
Young Man Singing. 1658. C. [No. 1144.]
Portrait of Himself. S. 1668. P. [No. 1143.]

COUNT SCHÖNBORN-BUCHHEIM.
Samson captured by the Philistines. S. 1636. C.

A. STRASSER.
Study of an Angel. 1655. P.

BELGIUM

ANTWERP, MUSEUM.
Portrait of Henry Swalm, known as "Portrait of a Burgomaster." S. 1637. C. [No. 705.]
The Young Fisher. S. 1659. P. [No. 294.]
Saskia. C. [No. 293.]
Portrait of an Old Jew. P. [No. 295.]

BRUSSELS, DUC D'ARENBERG.
Tobias curing his Father's Blindness. S. P.

COUNT MERODE-WESTERLOO.
St Peter repenting in Prison. S. 1631. P.

MUSEUM.
Portrait of a Man. S. 1641. C. [No. 397.]
Portrait of an Old Woman. S. 1654. P. [No. 397a.]

BRITISH ISLES

LONDON. NATIONAL GALLERY.
Portrait of an Old Woman. S. 1634. P. [No. 775.]
Portrait of a Man. S. 1635. C. [No. 850.]
Ecce Homo. Grisaille. 1636. C. [No. 1400.]
Portrait of Rembrandt. S. 1640. C. [No. 672.]
The Woman taken in Adultery. S. 1644. P. [No. 45.]
Adoration of the Shepherds. S. 1646. C. [No. 47.]
A Woman Bathing. S. 1654. P. [No. 54.]
Portrait of a Rabbi. S. 1657(?). C. [No. 190.]
Portrait of an Old Man. S. 1659. C. [No. 243.]
Portrait of a Monk. 1660. C. [No. 166.]
Portrait of Rembrandt. 1664. C. [No. 221.]
Portrait of a Woman. S. 1666. C. [No. 237.]
Portrait of a Jew Merchant. C. [No. 51.]
Landscape. P. [No. 72.]
Christ taken down from the Cross. P. [No. 43.]
Portrait of a Burgomaster. C. [No. 1674.]
Portrait of an Old Lady. C. [No. 1675.]

HERTFORD HOUSE COLLECTION.
Portrait of Burgomaster Pellicorne and his Son Caspar. S. 1632. C.
Suzanna van Collen, Wife of Pellicorne, and her Daughter. S. 1632. C.
The Good Samaritan. 1632. P.
Portrait of a Boy. S. 1633. Copper.
Portrait of Himself. S. 1633-1635. P.
Portrait of a Young Negro, known as the Black Archer. Oval. 1640. P.
Landscape. 1640. P.
Portrait of Himself. S. 1640. P.
Portrait of Himself. 1660.
Portrait of Titus. 1658. C.
The Unmerciful Servant. 1664. C.

BUCKINGHAM PALACE.
The Shipbuilder and his Wife. S. 1633. C. [No. 16.]
The Burgomaster Pancras and his Wife. Called Rembrandt and Saskia. S. 1635. C. [No. 30.]
Christ and Mary Magdalene at the Tomb. S. 1638. P. [No. 41.]
Portrait of a Lady. S. 1641. C. [No. 162.]
Portrait of Rembrandt. S. 164 – . P. [No. 174.]
The Adoration of the Magi. S. 1657. P. [No. 154.]
A Jewish Rabbi. C. [No. 131.]

HAMPTON COURT.
Portrait of a Rabbi. S. 1635. P. [No. 381.]

EDINBURGH. NATIONAL GALLERY.
A Young Woman in Bed. S. 1650. P.

DUBLIN. NATIONAL GALLERY.
Portrait of a Young Man. Said to be Louis van der Linden. 1631.
Shepherds reposing at Night. S. 1647. P. [No. 115.]
Descent From the Cross. S. 1650. C. Lent by the Duke of Abercorn.
Portrait of an Old Man. S. P. [No. 48.]

GLASGOW. CORPORATION GALLERIES.
The Slaughter-house. S. 16 – . P. [No. 707.]
Tobias and the Angel. 1654. P. [No. 705.]
A Man in Armour. S. 1655. C. [No. 706.]
The Painter's Study. P. [No. 709.]
Jeremiah mourning over the Destruction of Jerusalem. C. [No. 714.]

Study of an Old Man. P. [No. 711.]
Portrait of Rembrandt. P. [No. 710.]

HUNTERIAN MUSEUM.
Entombment. 1634. P.

CAMBRIDGE. FITZWILLIAM MUSEUM.
Portrait of Rembrandt. S. 1650. C. [No. 152.]

DULWICH COLLEGE.
A Young Man. S. 1632. P. [No. 189.]
A Young Girl at a Window. S. 1645. C. [No. 206.]

WINDSOR CASTLE.
A Young Man. S. 1631. P.
An Old Woman, known as the Countess of Desmond. 1631. P.

ALTHORP PARK. THE EARL SPENCER, K.G.
A Boy, formerly called a portrait of William III. P. 1660. C.
Woman with Flowers. 1660. C.
The Circumcision. P. 1661. C.
Rembrandt's Mother. C.

ASHRIDGE PARK. THE EARL BROWNLOW.
Portrait of a Jew. S. 1632. P.
Portrait of a Man, said to be Peter Cornelius van Hooft, the poet. S.
1653. C.
Isaac and Esau. P.
Landscape. A very doubtful picture. P.
Portrait of an Old Woman. C.

BASILDON PARK. CHARLES MORRISON.
Portrait of a Young Woman, called Rembrandt's daughter. S. 1665. C.

BELVOIR CASTLE. DUKE OF RUTLAND.
A Young Man. S. 1660. C.

BOWOOD. MARQUESS OF LANSDOWNE.
The Mill. 1654. C.

BRIGHTON. WILLIAM CHAMBERLIN.

Portrait of a Man-at-Arms. S. P.

BROOM HALL, DUNFERMLINE. LORD ELGIN.
Portrait of Saskia. S. 1633. P.

CANFORD MANOR, WIMBORNE. LORD WIMBORNE.
St Paul. S. 1658.
Portrait of a Man. 1660.

CASTLE HOWARD. THE EARL OF CARLISLE.
Portrait of a Young Artist drawing. S. 164 – . Life-size. 1648.

CHATSWORTH. DUKE OF DEVONSHIRE, K.G.
Portrait of a Rabbi. S. 1635. P.

DOWNTON CASTLE. A. R. BOUGHTON KNIGHT.
The Cradle. 1643-1645. P.
Portrait of a Man, known as "Rembrandt's Cook." S. 1661. C.
The Holy Family. P.

DRAYTON MANOR. SIR ROBERT PEEL.
The Finding of Moses. 1635. C. oval.

DUNCOMBE PARK. THE EARL OF FEVERSHAM.
A Merchant. S. 1659. C.

EDINBURGH. ARTHUR SANDERSON.
His Mother in a Hood. 1630. P.
Portrait of an Old Woman. S. 1635. C.

RICHARD SAUNDERSON (in 1836).
Abraham receiving the Angels.

GLASGOW. WILLIAM BEATTIE.
Study of Himself. 1629. P.

GOSFORD HOUSE. EARL OF WEMYSS AND MARCH.
A Monk reading. S. 1660. C.

THE GRANGE, ALRESFORD. LORD ASHBURTON.
Portrait of a Man. 1635. P.

Portrait of an Old Man. 1637. C.
Portrait of Lieven Willemsz van Coppenol. About 1650. P.
Portrait of Rembrandt. About 1658. C.
Portrait of a Man, said to be Cornelius Jansenius. P.

GRITTLETON. SIR A. D. NEELD, Bart.
Portrait of Rembrandt. S. 1660. C.
Portrait of a Burgomaster. S. P.

HINTON ST GEORGE. THE EARL POULETT.
Portrait of a Boy. S. 1628.

KEDDLESTON HALL. REV. LORD SCARSDALE.
Portrait of an Old Man. S. 1645. C.

KNOWSLEY HALL. THE EARL OF DERBY, K.G.
The Feast of Belshazzar. 1636. Doubtful Rembrandt. C.

LONDON. W. C. ALEXANDER.
Rembrandt's Mother. 1628. P.
The Painter's Sister. Doubtful. C.

WENTWORTH B. BEAUMONT.
The Tribute Money. S. 1645. C.

ALFRED BEIT.
St Francis Praying. S. 1637. P.
Portrait of a Young Man. 1660. C.

R. B. BERENS.
Portrait of the Painter. An early work. P.

BRIDGEWATER HOUSE. EARL OF ELLESMERE.
A Young Woman, aged 18. S. 1634. P.
A Young Woman. Oval. 1635.
Portrait of a Burgomaster, or, a Minister. S. 1637. C.
Hannah hearing the Young Samuel repeat his Prayers. S. 1648. P.
Study of an Old Man. 1655.
Portrait of Rembrandt. S. 165 – . C.

MONTAGUE HOUSE. DUKE OF BUCCLEUCH, K.G.
Portrait of Saskia. S. 1633. C.
Portrait of an Old Woman. S. 1655. C.
Portrait of Rembrandt. S. 1659. C.

BARONESS BURDETT-COUTTS.
A Forest Scene. P.

W. C. CARTWRIGHT.
Dead Peacocks. S. 1640. C.

THE EARL OF CRAWFORD, K.G.
Portrait of Titus. S. 1655. C.

THE EARL OF DERBY, K.G.
A Rabbi. S. 1635. P.
Joseph's Coat. 1647. C.

DEVONSHIRE HOUSE. THE DUKE OF DEVONSHIRE, K.G.
An Old Man. S. 1651. C.
An Old Man. S. 1652. C.

GEORGE C. W. FITZWILLIAM.
Portrait of a Man. 1632. P.

F. FLEISCHMANN.
Rembrandt's Father. S. 1631. P.

ALEXANDER HENDERSON.
Burgomaster Six. 1655. C.
Portrait of his Wife, Margaretha, Daughter of Dr. Tulp. S. 1655. P.

CAPTAIN HEYWOOD-LONSDALE.
Portrait of Rembrandt. S. 1635 or 8. P.

DORCHESTER HOUSE. CAPTAIN G. L. HOLFORD.
Martin Looten. S. 1632. P.
A Man with a Sword. S. 1644. C.
Portrait of a Lady, incorrectly called the wife of Jan Sylvius. 1645. C.
Portrait of Titus. S. 1660. C.

LORD FRANCIS PELHAM HOPE. (Collection sold in 1898.)
A Lady and Gentleman. S. 1633. C.
The Ship of St Peter. S. 1635. C.

THE EARL OF HOPETOUN.
Rembrandt's Mother. Oval. P.

R. W. HUDSON.
An Old Man. S. 1635. P.

THE EARL OF ILCHESTER.
Portrait of Rembrandt. S. 1658. C.

VICTORIA AND ALBERT MUSEUM.
Abraham dismissing Hagar and Ishmael. S. 1640. P.

LORD IVEAGH.
Portrait of a Woman. S. 1642. C.
Portrait of Rembrandt. 1663. C.

MRS JOSEPH.
Portrait of Saskia. S. 1636. P.

LESSER (1893).
Portrait of an Old Woman. S. 1635. C.

COLONEL LINDSAY (1893).
Portrait of a Very Old Woman. S. 1660. C.

MRS ALFRED MORRISON.
Portrait of Dr Bonus. S. 1642. C.

DUKE OF NEWCASTLE.
Portrait of an Orator. C.

THE EARL OF NORTHBROOK.
Landscape. 1640. P.
Portrait of an Old Man. S. 1667. C.

LORD PENRHYN.
Portrait of Catrina Hoogh. S. 1657. C.

JAMES REISS
Landscape. P.

MRS OWEN ROE.
Portrait of a Man. C.

LADY DE ROTHSCHILD.
Portrait of Rembrandt. S. 1656. C.

EDWARD H. SCOTT.
Rembrandt's Father's Mill. C.

COLONEL STERLING.
Portrait of a Man. C.

STEPHEN TUCKER.
The Angel departing from Tobit. P.

SIR CHARLES TURNER.
Portrait of a Girl. 1650. P.

LORD WANTAGE.
Portrait of an Old Woman. S. 1661. C.

T. HUMPHRY WARD.
An Old Man. 1630 or 1658. C.
A Young Man. S. 1646. C.
The Dismissal of Hagar. P.

GROSVENOR HOUSE. DUKE OF WESTMINSTER, K.G.
The Salutation. [No. 33.] S. 1640. P.
Portrait of a Gentleman with a Hawk. [No. 14.] S. 1643. C.
A Lady with a Fan. [No. 15.] S. 1643. C.
Portrait of Nicholas Berchem. [No. 19.] S. 1647. Cedar panel,
Portrait of his Wife. [No. 20], the daughter of Jan Wils. S. 1647. Cedar
panel,.
Portrait of Rembrandt. P.
Landscape. [No. 83.] P.

HENRY WILLETT.
Portrait of a Man. P.

SIR MATTHEW WILSON.
Portrait of a Lady. Oval. P.

THE EARL OF YARBOROUGH.
Portrait of an Old Lady. 1637. P.

NEW HALL, BODENHAM. ALFRED BUCKLEY.
Sketch of a Man's Head. P.

PANSHANGER. THE EARL COWPER, K.G.
Portrait of a Man. S. 1644. C.
Portrait of Marshal Turenne. 1649. C.
Head of a Man. P.

PETWORTH. LORD LECONFIELD.
Portrait of the Painter's Sister. S. 1631. P.
Portrait of Rembrandt. S. 1632. Oval. P.
Portrait of a Lady. S. 1635. C.
Portrait of a Youth. S. 1666. C.
Girl with a Rosebud. S. P.

RICHMOND. THE EXECUTORS OF THE LATE SIR FRANCIS
COOK.
The Painter's Sister. S. 1632. Oval. P.
Portrait of Alotte Adriaans, Wife of Elias Van Trip. S. 1639. P.
Tobit and His Wife. S. 1650. P.
Study of an Old Man. P.
The Prodigal Son. S. 1634. A very doubtful picture. C.

ROSSIE PRIORY, INCHTURE, PERTHSHIRE. LORD KINNAIRD.
Portrait of a Young Woman. S. 1636.
Portrait of Rembrandt. S. 1661. C.

WELBECK ABBEY, NOTTS. DUKE OF PORTLAND.
Head of a Boy. S. 1634. P.

WILTON HOUSE. THE EARL OF PEMBROKE.
An Old Woman Reading. S. 1631. C.

WOBURN ABBEY. DUKE OF BEDFORD.
Portrait of an Old Man. 1632.

Portrait of Rembrandt. 1635. C.

PRESENT OWNERS UNKNOWN.
Portrait of a Saint. S. 1635. C.
Portrait of a Lady. P.
Landscape. C.

DENMARK.

COPENHAGEN. NEW CARLSBERG GLYPTOTEK.
Man Reading. 1645. C.

COUNT MOLTKE.
Portrait of an Old Woman. [NO. 32.] 1654. C.

COPENHAGEN. MUSEUM.
Christ at Emmaus. [No. 292.] S. 1648. C.
Portrait of a Young Man. [No. 273.] S. 1656. C.
Portrait of a Young Woman. [No. 274.] Companion to the last. S. 1656.
C.

FRANCE.

PARIS. THE LOUVRE.
A Philosopher in Meditation. [No. 2540, Grand Gallery.] S. 1633. P.
A Philosopher in Meditation. [No. 2541, Grand Gallery.] 1633. P.
Portrait of Rembrandt. [No. 2552, Salle XV.] S. 1633. C.
Portrait of Rembrandt. [No. 2553, Grand Gallery.] S. 1634. P.
The Angel Raphael leaving Tobit. [No. 2536, Grand Gallery.] S. 1637.
P.
Portrait of Rembrandt. [No. 2554, Grand Gallery.] S. 1637. P.
Portrait of an Old Man. [No. 2544, Grand Gallery.] S. 1638. Oval. P.
The Carpenter's Home. [No. 2542, Salon Carré.] S. 1640. P.
A Woman Bathing. [No. 2550, Salle Lacaze.] 1647. P.
Christ at Emmaus. [No. 2539, Salon Carré.] S. 1648. P.
The Good Samaritan. [No. 2537, Grand Gallery.] S. 1648. P.
Portrait of a Man. [No. 2551, Salle Lacaze.] S. 1651. C.
Portrait of Hendrickje Stoffels. [No. 2547, Salon Carré.] P. about 1652.
C.
Bathsheba, or a Woman bathing. [No. 2549, Salle Lacaze.] S. 1654. C.
Portrait of a Man. [No. 2546, Grand Gallery.] 1655. P.

The Slaughter-house. [No. 2548, Grand Gallery.] S. 1655. P.
Portrait of a Young Man. [No. 2545, Salon Carré.] S. 1658. C.
Portrait of Rembrandt. [No. 2555, Salon Carré.] S. 1660. C.
Saint Matthew. [No. 2538, Grand Gallery.] S. 1661. C.
Venus and Cupid. [No. 2543, Grand Gallery.] 1661. C.

ÉPINAL. MUSEUM.
Portrait of an Old Woman. [No. 101.] S. 1661. C.

NANTES. MUSEUM.
Portrait of Rembrandt's Father. [No. 522, attributed to van Vliet.] 1628. P.

PARIS. MME. ANDRÉ-JACQUEMART.
Christ at Emmaus. S. R.H. 1629. Paper on panel
Portrait of Lysbeth van Rijn. S. 1632. C.
Portrait of Arnold Tholinx. S. 1656. C.

LÉON BONNAT.
Petitioners To a Biblical King. 1633. P.
Jean Six at a Window. Very doubtful. P.
Figure of Susannah. Oval. 1647. P.
Tasters in a Cellar. 1650. P.
Portrait of an Old Man. 1650. P.
Portrait of a Rabbi. 1655. P.
Head of an Old Man. 1660. P.

MARQUIS BONI DE CASTELLANE.
Portrait of Nicholas Ruts. S. 1631. P.

PRINCE DE CHALAIS.
Portrait of a Man.

LÉON GAUCHEZ.
Lucretia. S. 1664. C.

LEOPOLD GOLDSCHMIDT.
Portrait of a Woman. Called Rembrandt's cook. 1655. C.

HARJES.
Old Man With a White Beard. C.

BARONESS HIRSCH-GEREUTH (THE LATE).
Portrait of his Sister, or Saskia. Oval. S. 1633. P.

MAURICE KANN.
Head of Christ. 1660. C.
A Man in a Red Cloak. S. 1659. P.
Portrait of a Man. P. between 1666 and 1668. C.

RODOLPHE KANN.
Head of Christ. 1652. P
Portrait of Titus. S. 1655. C.
Portrait of a Rabbi. 1655. P.
Portrait of an Old Woman. S. 1657. P.
Old Woman cutting her Nails. S. 1658. C.
Portrait of a Young Woman. 1668. C.

MME. LACROIX.
Landscape, with Swans. 1645. C.

ALBERT LEHMANN.
Zachariah receiving the Prophecy of the Birth of John the Baptist. S.
1632. P.

PAUL MATHEY.
Head of an Old Man. P.

HENRY PEREIRE.
Portrait of a Man. S. 1632. P.
Portrait of Cornelia Pronck. Wife of the man. S. 1633. P.

JULES PORGÈS.
The Good Samaritan. S. 1639. C.
Portrait of a Rabbi. S. 1642. P.
An Old Woman meditating over a Book. 1649. C.
Portrait of Rembrandt's Brother. 1650. P.
Portrait of a Woman holding a Book. 1650. P.

COUNTESS EDMOND DE POURTALÈS.
Portrait of a Young Man rising from a Chair. S. 1633. C.

BARON ALPHONSE DE ROTHSCHILD.
Portrait of an Old Woman. S. 1632. P.

BARON GUSTAVE DE ROTHSCHILD.
Portrait of Martin Daey. S. 1634. C.
Portrait of Machteld van Doorn, Wife of Martin Daey. C.
The Standard-Bearer. S. 1636. C.

BARONESS NATHANIEL DE ROTHSCHILD.
Portrait of a Boy. S. 1633. P.

BARON N. DE ROTHSCHILD.
Portrait of Anthoni Copal. S. 1635. P.

DURAND RUEL.
David playing before Saul. 1663. C.

BARON ARTHUR DE SCHICKLER.
Judas with the Price of the Betrayal. 1629. C.

A. SCHLOSS.
Portrait of Saskia. Oval. 1634. P.
Old Man. S. 1643. P.

HENRI SCHNEIDER.
Hans Alenson. S. 1634. C.
The Wife of Alenson. S. 1634. C.

CHARLES SEDELMEYER.
Pilate washing his Hands. 1656. C.

CHARLES WALTNER.
An Old Rabbi. 1654-56. C.

E. WARNECK.
Diana bathing. 1631. P.
Rembrandt laughing. S. 1633. P.
Study of a Rabbi. 1650 To 1655. P
Study of a Young Boy. 1654. P.

DR MELVIL WASSERMANN.
Study of his Father. 1630. P.
Portrait of an Old Man. 1633. P.


ROUEN. M. DUTUIT.
Portrait of Rembrandt. S. 1631. P.


TOURS. MUSEUM.
Portrait of His Father. [No. 437.] A copy of the one in the Museum at
Nantes. 1628. P.


GERMANY.


BERLIN GALLERY. ROYAL MUSEUM.
The Money-Changer. [No. 828 D.] S. 1627. P.
Judith, or Minerva. [No. 828 C.] 1631. P.
The Rape of Proserpina. [No. 823.] 1632. P.
Rembrandt. [No. 810.] S. 1634. P.
Rembrandt. [No. 808.] 1634. P.
Samson threatening his Father-in-law [No. 802], formerly called The
Duke of Gueldres. S. 1635. C.
Portrait of the Minister Anslo consoling a Widow. S. 1641. C.
Portrait of Saskia. [No. 812.] S. 1643. P.
Portrait of a Rabbi. [No. 828 A.] S. 1645. C.
The Wife of Tobias with the Goat. [No. 805.] S. 1645. P.
Joseph's Dream. [No. 806.] S. 1645. P.
Susannah and the Elders. [No. 828 E.] S. 1647. P.
Daniel's Vision. [No. 828 F.] 1650. C.
Joseph accused by Potiphar's Wife. [No. 828 H.] S. 1655. C.
Study of an Old Man. [No. 828 J.] 1655. C.
John the Baptist preaching. [No. 828 K.] S. 1656. C.
Jacob Wrestling with the Angel. [No. 828.] S. 1659. C.
Moses breaking the Tables of the Law. [No. 811.] S. 1659. C.
Portrait of Hendrickje Stoffels. [No. 828 B.] 1662. C.


ALTFRANKEN. COUNT LUCKNER.
Portrait of Saskia. S. 1635. P.


ANHOLT. PRINCE OF SALM-SALM.
Diana, Actæon, and Callisto. S. 1635. C.

ASCHAFFENBOURG. ROYAL MUSEUM.
The Risen Christ. S. 1661. C.

BERLIN. VON CARSTANGEN.
Portrait of J. C. Sylvius. S. 1645. C.
Christ at the Column. 1646. P.
Portrait of Rembrandt. S. 1665. C.

EMPEROR FREDERICK MUSEUM.
Rembrandt's Brother. 1650. C.

CARL HOLLITSCHER.
St Paul in Meditation. 1635. C.
Christ on the Cross. 1648. P.

ROBERT VON MENDELSSOHN.
Rembrandt. S. 1651. P.

SANS-SOUCI.
The Capture of Samson. S. 1628. P.

JAMES SIMON.
Portrait of a Young Girl. S. 1634. P.

BONN. PROFESSOR G. MARTIUS.
An Old Woman. 1640. P.

BRUNSWICK. GRAND DUCAL MUSEUM.
An Unknown Man. [No. 232.] 1631. P.
Portrait of a Woman. [No. 233.] S. 1633. P.
Portrait of a Man. [No. 237.] S. 1638. P.
Stormy Landscape. [No. 236.] S. 1640. P.
Noli Me Tangere. [No. 235.] S. 1651. C.
Portrait of a Family. [No. 238] S. 1668. C.

CARLSRUHE. GRAND DUCAL MUSEUM.
Portrait of Himself. [No. 238.] S. 1645. P.

CASSEL. MUSEUM.
Rembrandt. [No. 208.] 1627. P.
An Old Man. [No. 209.] S. 1630. P.

An Old Man. [No. 210.] S. 1632. P.
An Old Man. [No. 211.] S. 1632. P.
Portrait, said to be Coppenol. [No. 212.] S. 1632. C.
Jan Herman Krul. [No. 213.] S. 1633. C.
Saskia. [No. 214.] 1634. P.
Rembrandt. [No. 215.] S. 1634. P.
A Young Woman. [No. 216.] 1635. P.
A Man. [No. 217.] S. 1639. C.
Holy Family. [No. 218.] Called "The Woodchopper." S. 1646. P.
A Winter Landscape. [No. 219.] S. 1646. P.
The Ruin. [No. 220.] S. 1650. P.
Portrait of Bruyningh. [No. 221.] S. 1652. C.
Man in Armour, known as "The Watch." [No. 223.] S. 1655. C.
An Old Man. [No. 226.] 1655. P.
An Old Man. [No. 225.] 1657. P.
An Architect, or Geometrician. [No. 224.] 1656. C.
Jacob Blessing Joseph's Sons. [No. 227.] S. 1656. C.
Portrait of Rembrandt. [No. 222.] S. 1659. C.


COLOGNE. BARON A. VON OPPENHEIM.
A Young Girl. 1655. P.


DARMSTADT. GRAND-DUCAL GALLERY.
The Flagellation. [No. 347.] S. 1668. C.


DRESDEN. ROYAL GALLERY.
Saskia. [No. 1556.] S. 1633. P.
A Man. [No. 1557.] Willem Burchgraeff. [No. 182.] S. 1633. P.
The Capture of Ganymede. [No. 1558.] S. 1635. C.
Rembrandt and Saskia. [No. 1559.] S. 1635. C.
The Marriage of Samson. [No. 1560.] S. 1638. C.
The Man with the Bittern. [No. 1661.] S. 1639. P.
Saskia holding a Pink. [No. 1562.] S. 1641. P.
The Sacrifice of Manoah. [No. 1563.] S. 1641. C.
Old Woman weighing Gold. [No. 1564.] C.
A Young Man. [No. 1565.] S. 1643. C.
An Old Man. [No. 1571.] 1645. C.
The Entombment. [No. 1566.] S. 1653. C.
An Old Man with a Beard. [No. 1567.] S. 1654. P.
Portrait of a Man. [No. 1568.] 1656.
Rembrandt. [No. 1569.] S. 1657.

An Old Man. [No. 1570.] 1666.

ELBERFELD. KARL VON DER HEYDT.
The Denial of St Peter. S. 1628. Copper.
A Lady. S. 1635. P.

FRANKFORT. STÆDEL ART INSTITUTE.
David playing before Saul. [No. 183.] P.
Portrait of Margaretha van Bilderbeecq. [No. 182.] Oval. S. 1633. P.
Parable of the Labourers in the Vineyard. [No. 181.] S. 1656. C.

GOTHA. MUSEUM.
Rembrandt. [No. 181.] S. 1629. P.

HAMBURG. KUNST-HALLE.
Maurice Huygens. S. 1632. C.

CONSUL WEBER.
Presentation in the Temple. S. 1630. P.
The Woman taken in Adultery. 1644. C.
A Pilgrim at Prayer. S. 1661.

LEIPZIG. JULIUS O. GOTTCHALD.
Study of an Old Man. 1630. P.

MUSEUM.
Rembrandt. [No. 347.] 1654. P.

ALFRED THIEME.
The Good Samaritan. 1640. C.
Portrait called the Constable of Bourbon. S. 1644.

METZ. MUSEUM.
An Old Man. S. 1633. P.

MUNICH. ROYAL GALLERY.
Holy Family. [No. 324.] S. 1631. C.
Portrait of a Turk. [No. 325.] S. 1633. P.
The Descent from the Cross. [No. 326.] S. 1633. P.
The Elevation of the Cross. [No. 327.] 1633.
The Ascension. [No. 328.] S. 1636.

The Entombment. [No. 330.] 1638.
The Resurrection. [No. 329.] S. 1639.
The Adoration of the Shepherds. [No. 331.] S. 1646.
Rembrandt. [No. 333.] S. 1654. P.

DR MARTIN SCHUBART.
An Old Man. 1632. P.

NORDKIRCHEN. COUNT ESTERHAZY.
A Young Man. S. 1629.

NUREMBERG. MUSEUM.
Rembrandt [No. 298], in armour. S. 1629. P.
Saint Paul. 1629.

OLDENBURG. AUGUSTEUM.
The Prophetess Anna, or the painter's mother. [No. 166.] S. 1631.
An Old Man. [No. 167.] S. 1632.
Landscape. [No. 169.] 1645. P.

POSEN. COUNT EDWARD RACZYNSKI.
Christ. S. 1661.

SCHWERIN. GRAND DUCAL MUSEUM.
An Old Man. [No. 854.] S. 1630. P.
An Old Man. [No. 855.] 1656.

STRASBURG. MUSEUM.
An Old Man, holding a scroll. 1650.

STUTTGART. MUSEUM.
St Paul in Prison. [No. 225.] S. 1627. P.

WEIMAR. GRAND DUKE OF SAXE-WEIMAR.
Portrait of Rembrandt. S. 1643.

HOLLAND.

THE HAGUE. MAURITSHUIS, ROYAL MUSEUM.
Rembrandt's Mother. [No. 556, Room XIV.] 1628. P.
Rembrandt's Father. [No. 565, Room XIV.] 1628. P.

Rembrandt. [No. 148, Room XIV.] 1629. P.

A Man Laughing. [No. 598, Room XIV.] 1630. P.

A Young Girl. [No. 577, Room XIV.] S. 1630. P.

The Presentation in the Temple. [No. 145, Room XIV.] S. 1631. P.

The Anatomy Lesson of Professor Pieterszoon Tulp. [No. 146, Room XIII.] S. 1632. C.

Rembrandt As an Officer. [No. 149, Room XIV.] S. 1634. P.

The Flight Into Egypt. [No. 579, Room XIV.] S. 1636. P.

A Woman at Her Toilet. [No. 552, Room XIV.] S. 1637. P.

Susannah at the Bath. [No. 147, Room XIV.] S. 1637. P.

Portrait Believed To Be Rembrandt's Brother Adriaen. [No. 560, Room XIV.] S. 1650.

Homer Reciting His Poems. [No. 584, Room XIV.] S. 1663. C.


AMSTERDAM. RYKSMUSEUM.
Rembrandt's Father. [No. 1248.] 1629.

A Young Lady, Known As the Lady of Utrecht. S. 1639. P.

Elizabeth Bas [No. 1249], Widow of Admiral Swartenhout. 1640. C.

The Sortie of the Company of Captain Frans Banning Cocq [No. 1246], Called "the Night Watch." S. 1642. C.

Mythological Subject. [No. 1251.] 1650.

The Anatomy Lesson of Dr Johannes Deyman. [No. 1250.] S. 1656. C.

The Syndics of the Drapers. [No. 1247.] S. 1661. C.

The Jewish Bride. [No. 1252.] S. 1665. C.


DR C. HOFSTEDE DE GROOT.
Rembrandt's Sister. 1630. P.


SIX COLLECTION.
Joseph Interpreting His Dreams. S. 1630. Cardboard.

Anna Vymer. S. 1641. P.

Portrait of Ephraim Bonus. 1647. P.

Burgomaster Six. 1660. C.


THE HAGUE. DR BREDIUS.
A Woman Praying. 1654. P.


PRINCE HENRI DES PAYS-BAS.
Rembrandt. S. 1643.

D. F. SCHEURLEER.
Head of a Boy. 1629.

STEENGRACHT COLLECTION.
The Toilet of Bathsheba. S. 1643. P.

LEEUWARDEN. BARON VAN HARINXMA THOE SLOOTEN.
Portrait of an Old Man. S. 1644. P.

ROTTERDAM. BOYMANS MUSEUM.
Portrait of Rembrandt's Father. [No. 237, Room B.] S. 1630. Oval. P.
The Peace of the Country. [No. 238, Room D.] S. 1640. P.

ITALY.

FLORENCE. PITTI PALACE.
Rembrandt. [No. 60, Room 5.] 1635.
An Old Man. [No. 16, Room 6.] S. 1658. C.

UFFIZI.
Portrait of Rembrandt. [No. 451, Room 13.] 1655.
Portrait of Rembrandt. [No. 452, Room 13.] 1666.

SIGNOR FABRI.
Study of an Old Man. P.

MILAN. BRERA.
A Woman. [No. 449.] S. 1632. P.

ROUMANIA.

SINAIA. THE KING OF ROUMANIA.
Esther, Haman, and Ahasuerus. 1668. C.

RUSSIA.

ST PETERSBURG. THE HERMITAGE.
Portrait of Rembrandt's Father. [No. 814.] S. 1630. P.
Portrait of a Man. [No. 808.] S. 1631. C.
The Descent From the Cross. [No. 800.] S. 1634. C.
The Incredulity of St Thomas. [No. 801.] S. 1634. P.

The Jewish Bride. [No. 812.] S. 1634. C.
A Young Man [No. 828]. S. 1634. P.
The Sacrifice of Isaac. [No. 792.] S. 1635. C.
Portrait of an Oriental. [No. 813.] S. 1636.
Danae. [No. 892.] S. 1636. C.
Portrait of a Man, called Sobieski. [No. 811.] S. 1637. P.
The Parable of the Master of the Vineyard. [No. 798.] S. 1637. P.
An Old Woman. [No. 829.] S. 1643. P.
The Reconciliation of David and Absalom. [No.1777.] S. 1642. P.
Rembrandt's Mother. [No. 807.] S. 1643. P.
The Holy Family. [No. 796.] S. 1645. C.
Portrait of a Man, erroneously called Manasseh Ben Israel. [No. 820.]
S. 1645. C.
Abraham Receiving the Angels. [No. 791.] 1650. C.
The Sons of Jacob showing him Joseph's Coat. [No. 793.] S. 1650. C.
The Disgrace of Haman. [No. 795.] S. 1650. C.
Pallas. [No. 809.] 1650. C.
Hannah Teaching the Infant Samuel to Read. [No. 822.] S. 1650. C.
Girl with a Broom. [No. 826.] S. 1651. C.
An Old Woman. [No. 804.] 1654. C.
An Old Woman. [No. 805.] S. 1654. C.
An Old Woman. [No. 806.] S. 1654. C.
An Old Jew. [No. 810.] S. 1654. C.
An Old Man. [No. 818.] 1654. C.
An Old Man. [No. 823.] S. 1654. C.
An Old Man. [No. 824.] S. 1654. C.
Joseph Accused by Potiphar's Wife. [No. 794.] S. 1655. C.
St Peter's Denial. [No. 799.] S. 1656. C.
A Young Woman. [No. 819.] S. 1656. C.
Young Woman trying on an Earring. [No. 817.] S. 1657. P.
A Young Man. [No. 825.] 1660. C.
Portrait of a Man. [No. 821.] S. 1661. C.
Portrait of Jeremias de Decker, the Poet. [No. 827.] S. 1666. P.
The Prodigal Son. [No. 797.] 1669. C.
An Old Jew. [No. 815.] S. P.

PRINCE JOUSOUPOFF.
Head of a Young Boy. S. 1633. P.
Susannah and the Elders. S. 1637.
A Young Man. 1660. C.
A Lady With an Ostrich Feather. 1660. C.

PRINCE OF LEUCHTEMBERG.
Rembrandt. [No. 108]. 1643. P.


COUNT A. W. ORLOFF-DAVIDOFF.
Christ. 1660. C.


COUNT S. STROGANOFF.
A Philosopher in Meditation. S. 1630. P.
A Young Monk. S. 1660. C.


SPAIN.


MADRID. PRADO.
Queen Artemisia receiving the Ashes of Mausolus. [No. 1544.]
Otherwise Known As Cleopatra at her toilet. S. 1634. C.


SWEDEN.


STOCKHOLM. ROYAL MUSEUM.
A Young Girl. [No. 591.] 1630. P.
St Anastasius. [No. 579.] S. 1631. P.
Saskia. [No. 583.] S. 1632.
Study of an Old Man as St Peter. [No. 1349.] S. 1632.
An Old Man. [No. 585.] S. 1633.
The Young Servant. S. 1654.
An Old Man. [No. 581.] S. 1655.
An Old Woman. [No. 582.] S. 1655.
The Conspiracy of Claudius Civilis. [No. 578.] 1661. C.


VANAS. COUNT AXEL DE WACHTMEISTER.
A Young Man. S. 1632. P.
A Young Man. 1643. C.


UNITED STATES OF AMERICA.


CHICAGO. ARMOUR.
Portrait of a Man. S. 1643.


P. C. HANFORD.
An Accountant by a Table. C.

NEW YORK. W. H. BEERS.
Rembrandt's Father. 1632.

ROBERT W. DE FOREST.
Head of a Young Man.

H. O. HAVEMEYER.
Portrait of Christian Paul van Beersteyn, Burgomaster of Delft. S.
1632.
Portrait of Volkera Nicolai Knobbert, wife of Beersteyn. S. 1632.
Portrait of Paulus Doomer, called "The Gilder." S. 1640. P.
A Woman, aged 87. S. 1640 or 1646.

ROBERT HOE.
Young Gipsy holding a Medallion. 1650. C.

MORRIS K. JESSUP.
Portrait of a Young Man, erroneously called Six.
Portrait of his Wife.

METROPOLITAN MUSEUM.
A Man. [no. 277.] 1640.
An Old Man. [no. 274.] S. 1665.
The Mills. [no. 276.]
The Adoration of the Shepherds. [No. 278.] P.

J. PIERPONT MORGAN.
Portrait of Rembrandt. C.

R. MORTIMER.
Portrait of a Young Man putting on His Armour. 1634. C.

W. SCHAUS.
Portrait of an Admiral, erroneously called "Van Tromp." 1658. P.

CHARLES STEWART SMITH.
St John. Oval. S. 1632. P.

C. T. YERKES.
The Raising of Lazarus. 1628. P.
Joris de Caulery. S. 1632.

Portrait of a Rabbi. 1635. P.
Philemon and Baucis. S. 1658. P.

PHILADELPHIA. P. A. B. WIDENER.
Portrait of Saskia. 1633. P.
PITTSBURGH. A. M. BYERS.
Portrait of Saskia. S. 1636. P.

SAN FRANCISCO. WILLIAM H. CROCKER.
Portrait of a Young Boy. P.

UNKNOWN OWNERS.
A Young Man, Called Tulp. S. 1634. P.
Portrait of a Young Woman. S. 1634. P.
A Man, called Matthys Kalkoen. S. 1632. C.
Portrait of Saskia. S. 1634.
Portrait called "The Dutch Admiral." S. 1643.
Portrait of a Lady. S. 1643.
An Orphan Girl of Amsterdam. S. 1645. C.
"The Standard-Bearer." 1662. C.
Portrait Called Six. S. C.

## ARTS, PAINTING, SCULPTURE

The Art of Andy Goldsworthy
Andy Goldsworthy: Touching Nature
Andy Goldsworthy in Close-Up
Andy Goldsworthy: Pocket Guide
Andy Goldsworthy In America
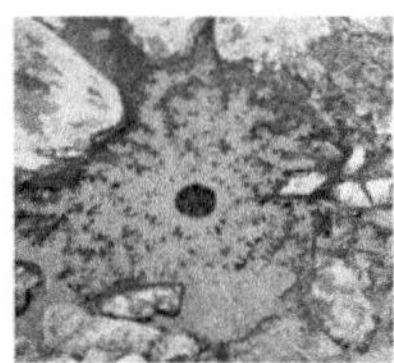
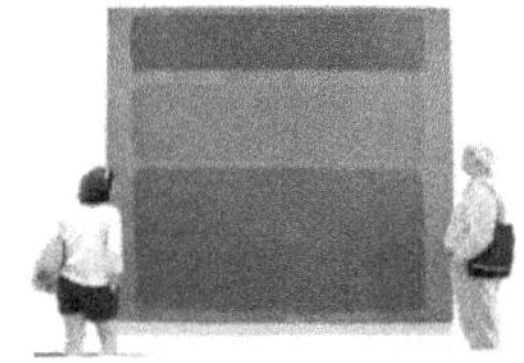
Land Art: A Complete Guide
The Art of Richard Long
Richard Long: Pocket Guide
Land Art In the UK
Land Art in Close-Up
Land Art In the U.S.A.
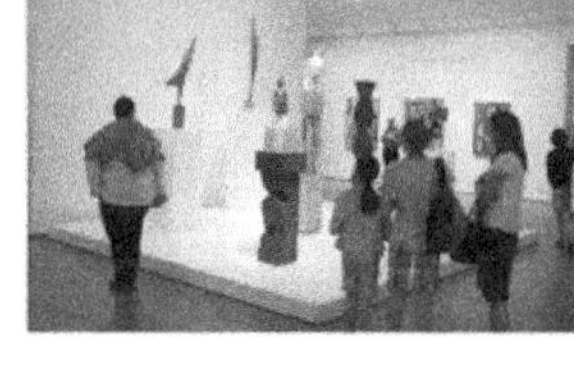
Land Art: Pocket Guide
Installation Art in Close-Up
Minimal Art and Artists In the 1960s and After
Colourfield Painting
Land Art DVD, TV documentary
Andy Goldsworthy DVD, TV documentary
The Erotic Object: Sexuality in Sculpture From Prehistory to the Present Day
Sex in Art: Pornography and Pleasure in Painting and Sculpture
Postwar Art
Sacred Gardens: The Garden in Myth, Religion and Art
Glorification: Religious Abstraction in Renaissance and 20th Century Art
Early Netherlandish Painting
Leonardo da Vinci
Piero della Francesca
Giovanni Bellini
Fra Angelico: Art and Religion in the Renaissance
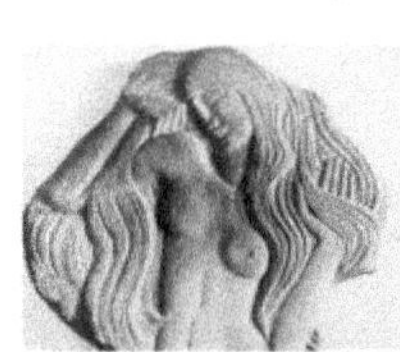
Mark Rothko: The Art of Transcendence
Frank Stella: American Abstract Artist
Jasper Johns
Brice Marden
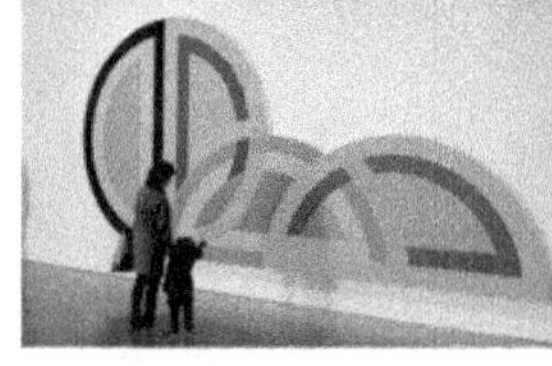
Alison Wilding: The Embrace of Sculpture
Vincent van Gogh: Visionary Landscapes
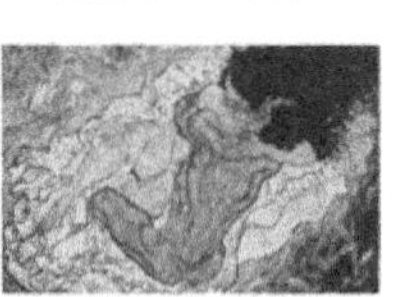
Eric Gill: Nuptials of God
Constantin Brancusi: Sculpting the Essence of Things
Max Beckmann
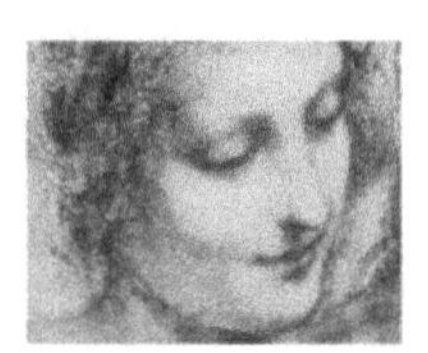
Caravaggio
Gustave Moreau
Egon Schiele: Sex and Death In Purple Stockings
Delizioso Fotografico Fervore: Works In Process 1
Sacro Cuore: Works In Process 2
The Light Eternal: J.M.W. Turner
The Madonna Glorified: Karen Arthurs
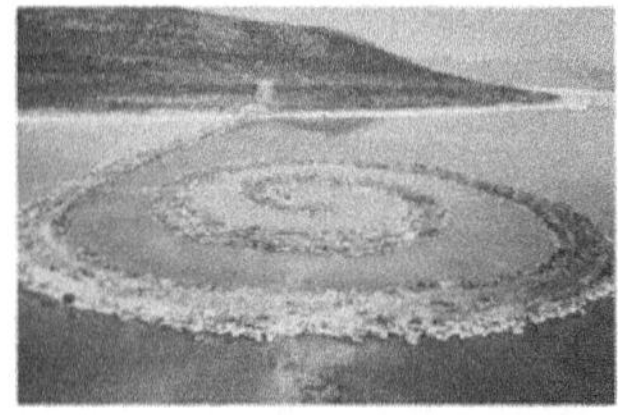

LITERATURE

J.R.R. Tolkien: The Books, The Films, The Whole Cultural Phenomenon
J.R.R. Tolkien: Pocket Guide
Tolkien's Heroic Quest
The *Earthsea* Books of Ursula Le Guin
Beauties, Beasts and Enchantment: Classic French Fairy Tales
German Popular Stories by the Brothers Grimm
Philip Pullman and *His Dark Materials*
Sexing Hardy: Thomas Hardy and Feminism
Thomas Hardy's *Tess of the d'Urbervilles*
Thomas Hardy's *Jude the Obscure*
Thomas Hardy: The Tragic Novels
Love and Tragedy: Thomas Hardy
The Poetry of Landscape in Hardy
Wessex Revisited: Thomas Hardy and John Cowper Powys
Wolfgang Iser: Essays and Interviews
Petrarch, Dante and the Troubadours
Maurice Sendak and the Art of Children's Book Illustration
Andrea Dworkin
Cixous, Irigaray, Kristeva: The *Jouissance* of French Feminism
Julia Kristeva: Art, Love, Melancholy, Philosophy, Semiotics and Psychoanalysis
Hélène Cixous I Love You: The *Jouissance* of Writing
Luce Irigaray: Lips, Kissing, and the Politics of Sexual Difference
Peter Redgrove: Here Comes the Flood
Peter Redgrove: Sex-Magic-Poetry-Cornwall
Lawrence Durrell: Between Love and Death, East and West
Love, Culture & Poetry: Lawrence Durrell
Cavafy: Anatomy of a Soul
German Romantic Poetry: Goethe, Novalis, Heine, Hölderlin
Feminism and Shakespeare
Shakespeare: Love, Poetry & Magic
The Passion of D.H. Lawrence
D.H. Lawrence: Symbolic Landscapes
D.H. Lawrence: Infinite Sensual Violence
Rimbaud: Arthur Rimbaud and the Magic of Poetry
The Ecstasies of John Cowper Powys
Sensualism and Mythology: The Wessex Novels of John Cowper Powys
Amorous Life: John Cowper Powys and the Manifestation of Affectivity  (H.W. Fawkner)
Postmodern Powys: New Essays on John Cowper Powys (Joe Boulter)
Rethinking Powys: Critical Essays on John Cowper Powys
Paul Bowles & Bernardo Bertolucci
Rainer Maria Rilke
Joseph Conrad: *Heart of Darkness*
In the Dim Void: Samuel Beckett
Samuel Beckett Goes into the Silence
André Gide: Fiction and Fervour
Jackie Collins and the Blockbuster Novel
Blinded By Her Light: The Love-Poetry of Robert Graves
The Passion of Colours: Travels In Mediterranean Lands
Poetic Forms

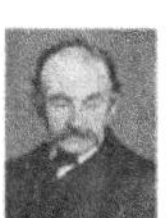
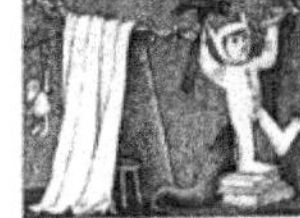
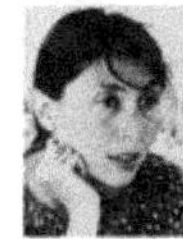
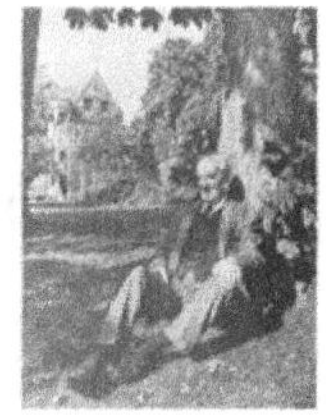
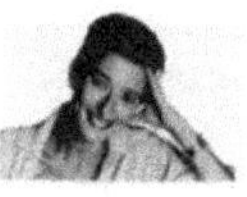
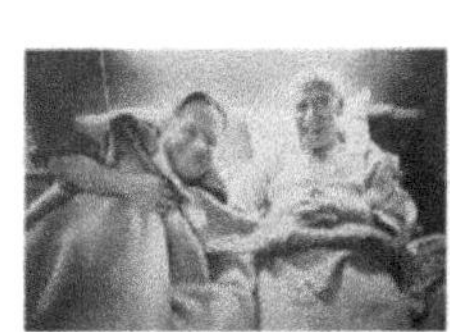
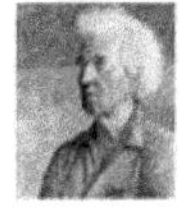
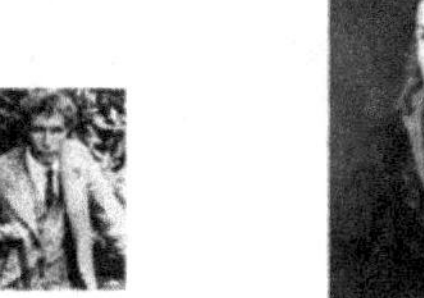
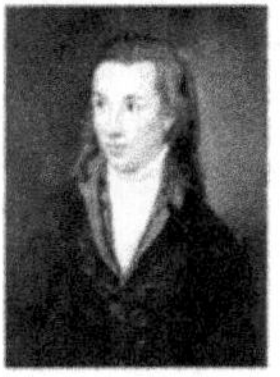

POETRY

Ursula Le Guin: Walking In Cornwall
Peter Redgrove: Here Comes The Flood
Peter Redgrove: Sex-Magic-Poetry-Cornwall
Dante: Selections From the Vita Nuova
Petrarch, Dante and the Troubadours
William Shakespeare: Sonnets
William Shakespeare: Complete Poems
Blinded By Her Light: The Love-Poetry of Robert Graves
Emily Dickinson: Selected Poems
Emily Brontë: Poems
Thomas Hardy: Selected Poems
Percy Bysshe Shelley: Poems
John Keats: Selected Poems
Joh n Keats: Poems of 1820
D.H. Lawrence: Selected Poems
Edmund Spenser: Poems
Edmund Spenser: Amoretti
John Donne: Poems
Henry Vaughan: Poems
Sir Thomas Wyatt: Poems
Robert Herrick: Selected Poems
Rilke: Space, Essence and Angels in the Poetry of Rainer Maria Rilke
Rainer Maria Rilke: Selected Poems
Friedrich Hölderlin: Selected Poems
Arseny Tarkovsky: Selected Poems
Arthur Rimbaud: Selected Poems
Arthur Rimbaud: A Season in Hell
Arthur Rimbaud and the Magic of Poetry
Novalis: Hymns To the Night
German Romantic Poetry
Paul Verlaine: Selected Poems
Elizaethan Sonnet Cycles
D.J. Enright: By-Blows
Jeremy Reed: Brigitte's Blue Heart
Jeremy Reed: Claudia Schiffer's Red Shoes
Gorgeous Little Orpheus
Radiance: New Poems
Crescent Moon Book of Nature Poetry
Crescent Moon Book of Love Poetry
Crescent Moon Book of Mystical Poetry
Crescent Moon Book of Elizabethan Love Poetry
Crescent Moon Book of Metaphysical Poetry
Crescent Moon Book of Romantic Poetry
Pagan America: New American Poetry

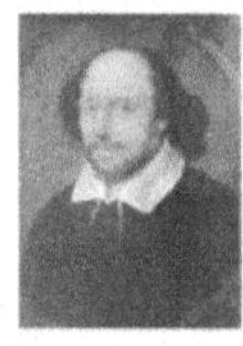
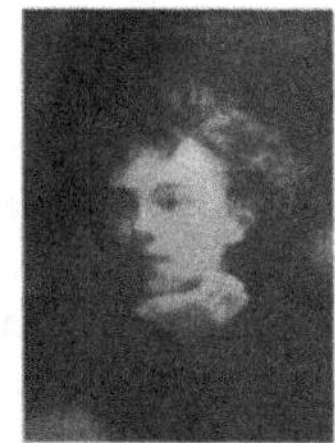
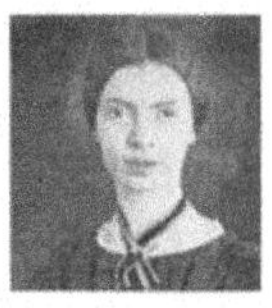
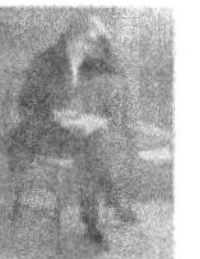
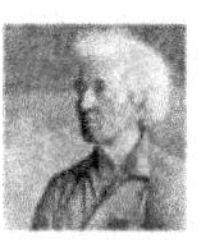
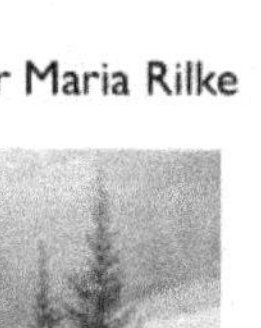
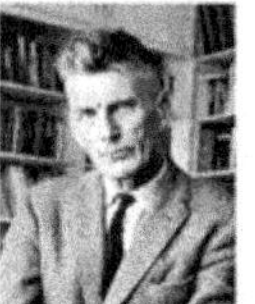
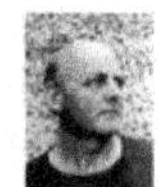
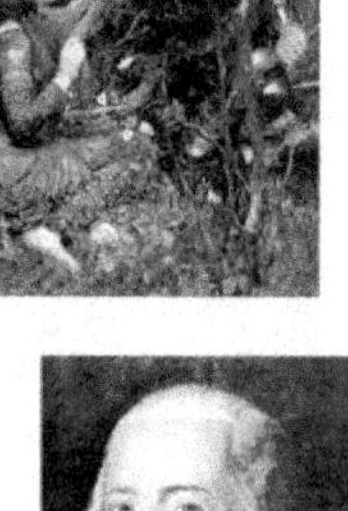
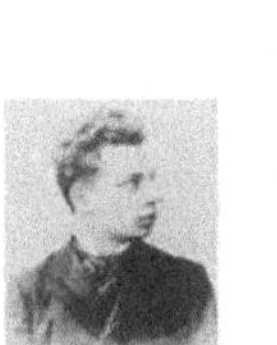
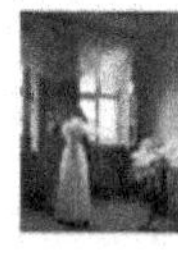
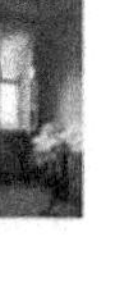

## MEDIA, CINEMA, FEMINISM and CULTURAL STUDIES

J.R.R. Tolkien: The Books, The Films, The Whole Cultural Phenomenon
J.R.R. Tolkien: Pocket Guide
The *Lord of the Rings* Movies: Pocket Guide
The Cinema of Hayao Miyazaki
Hayao Miyazaki: *Princess Mononoke*: Pocket Movie Guide
Hayao Miyazaki: *Spirited Away*: Pocket Movie Guide
Tim Burton : Hallowe'en For Hollywood
Ken Russell
Ken Russell: *Tommy*: Pocket Movie Guide
The Ghost Dance: The Origins of Religion
The Peyote Cult
Cixous, Irigaray, Kristeva: The *Jouissance* of French Feminism
Julia Kristeva: Art, Love, Melancholy, Philosophy, Semiotics and Psychoanalysis
Luce Irigaray: Lips, Kissing, and the Politics of Sexual Difference
Hélène Cixous I Love You: The *Jouissance* of Writing
Andrea Dworkin
'Cosmo Woman': The World of Women's Magazines
Women in Pop Music
HomeGround: The Kate Bush Anthology
Discovering the Goddess (Geoffrey Ashe)
The Poetry of Cinema
The Sacred Cinema of Andrei Tarkovsky
Andrei Tarkovsky: Pocket Guide
Andrei Tarkovsky: *Mirror*: Pocket Movie Guide
Andrei Tarkovsky: *The Sacrifice*: Pocket Movie Guide
Walerian Borowczyk: Cinema of Erotic Dreams
Jean-Luc Godard: The Passion of Cinema
Jean-Luc Godard: *Hail Mary*: Pocket Movie Guide
Jean-Luc Godard: *Contempt*: Pocket Movie Guide
Jean-Luc Godard: *Pierrot le Fou*: Pocket Movie Guide
John Hughes and Eighties Cinema
*Ferris Bueller's Day Off*: Pocket Movie Guide
Jean-Luc Godard: Pocket Guide
The Cinema of Richard Linklater
Liv Tyler: Star In Ascendance
*Blade Runner* and the Films of Philip K. Dick
Paul Bowles and Bernardo Bertolucci
Media Hell: Radio, TV and the Press
An Open Letter to the BBC
Detonation Britain: Nuclear War in the UK
Feminism and Shakespeare
Wild Zones: Pornography, Art and Feminism
Sex in Art: Pornography and Pleasure in Painting and Sculpture
Sexing Hardy: Thomas Hardy and Feminism

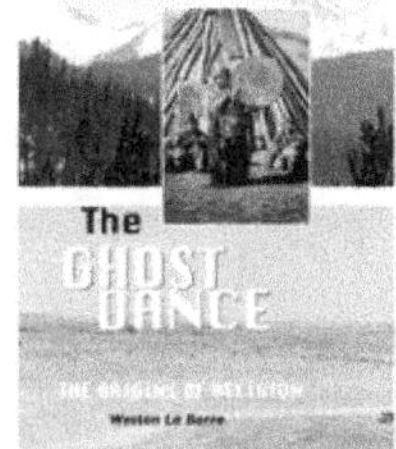
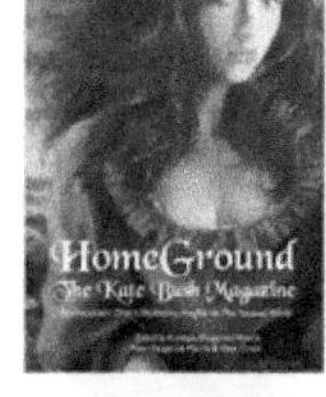
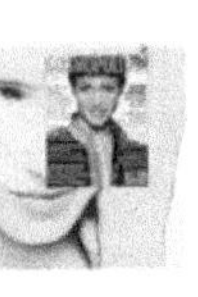
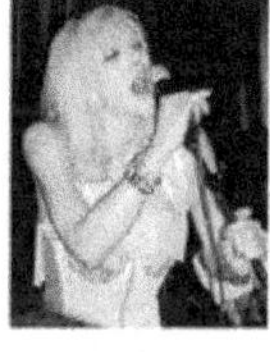
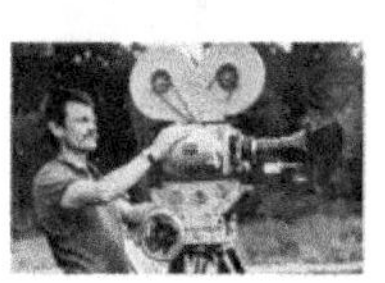
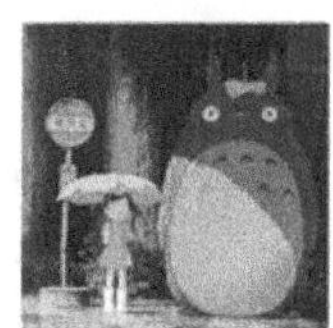
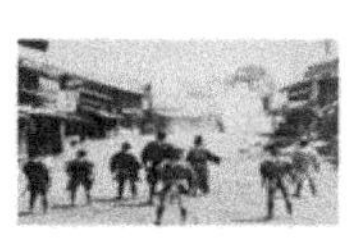
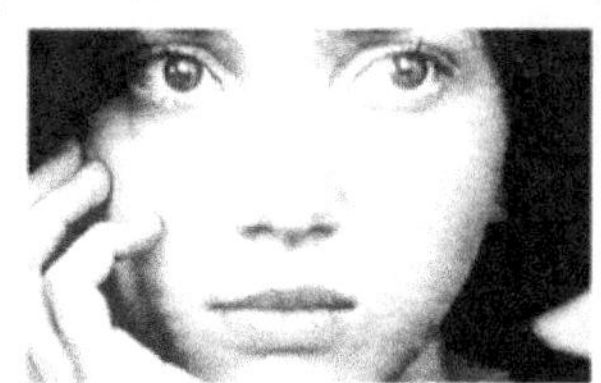
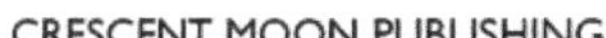

*The Light Eternal* is a model monograph, an exemplary job. The subject matter of the book is beautifully
organised and dead on beam. (Lawrence Durrell)
It is amazing for me to see my work treated with such passion and respect. (Andrea Dworkin)


CRESCENT MOON PUBLISHING
P.O. Box 1312, Maidstone, Kent, ME14 5XU, Great Britain. www.crmoon.com

cresmopub@yahoo.co.uk   www.crescentmoon.org.uk